The Archive of James Russell, Garden Designer

Deposited at the Borthwick Institute, University of York

Katrina Legg

© UNIVERSITY OF YORK, 2003

ISBN 1-904497-07-1

Contents

James Russell Archive

Acknowledgements	*iii*
Life & Works	*v*
Administrative History	*xv*
Access	*xx*
James Russell Papers: Archive List	*1*
Index	*81*

ACKNOWLEDGEMENTS

This project, to preserve and catalogue the James Russell archive, owes its inception to Peter Goodchild's identification of the value of the material, and his persuading James Russell of that value. The task of raising sufficient funds to complete the necessary work was shouldered, and successfully completed, by Helen Lazenby, Karen Lynch and Val Hepworth. Without their hard work, and the support of The Yorkshire Gardens Trust over many months, the archive would not today be preserved and catalogued. The generosity of individuals, the John Spedan Lewis Foundation and the Stanley Smith (UK) Horticultural Trust provided the funds for the preservation and cataloguing to be carried out.

Katrina Legg, whose name appears as the author of this catalogue, did the work of cataloguing the archive, and of identifying and rectifying preservation problems. Katrina was supported by her colleagues in the Borthwick Institute, especially Christopher Webb, the staff of the conservation department, Trevor Cooper and Alison Fairburn, and Sara Slinn, who completed the typesetting of the manuscript. Eton College archive helped with information about Russell's academic career at Eton.

Jane Russell, Jim's sister, has maintained a close interest in the project throughout, and provided invaluable insights into the life and career of a remarkable plantsman.

JAMES RUSSELL: LIFE & WORKS

Childhood and Education

James Philip Cuming Russell was born into a military family on 3 April 1920. Despite his father's occupation, and the expectation that Russell would either follow in his father's footsteps or enter the diplomatic service, Russell went onto pursue his love of plants and gardening to become, in the eyes of many, one of the most influential landscape gardeners of his time.

Following his education at preparatory school Russell attended Eton, where his interest in plants continued to grow, winning the Harmsworth Memorial Prize for drawing in the flowers class in the summer of 1935. While at Eton he made friends and connections that were to stand him in good stead through his later life, including his friendship with George Howard. After leaving Eton in 1938 Russell spent some time visiting gardens both in Britain and on the Continent. Russell intended this period to be a preparation for reading botany at Cambridge, but his plans were disrupted by the outbreak of World War II. He was commissioned in the Hertfordshire Yeomanry and in 1942 he was invalided out of the armed services, resumed a civilian life and the career he had originally wished for.

Sunningdale Nurseries, Windlesham, Surrey and Garden Design

Following his discharge, Russell become involved with Sunningdale Nurseries. The nursery had been acquired by his father and cousin from Sir Hubert Longman shortly before the war. This famous nursery, which had been founded in 1846, had fallen into a poor state of repair by the time Russell took up the helm, reorganising and restoring it to its former glory, as 'The most beautiful nursery in Britain'.[1] The rhododendron collection, a species that Russell became associated with, had been introduced 'by Hooker from Sikkim as well as many of Fortune's

---

[1] For a brief article about the nursery by James Russell see the *Journal of the Royal Horticultural Society*, January 1958, vol. 83, part 1, pp. 15-23.

JAMES RUSSELL: LIFE AND WORKS

Japanese collections'[2] and proved a focal point in both the resuscitation of the nursery and later for the creation of Ray Wood at Castle Howard.

In 1950 Russell began designing a landscape for Seaton Delaval, Northumberland for Lord Hastings[3] and from there on he was drawn away from the nursery at Sunningdale becoming more concerned with garden design. Lord Hastings was the first in a large number of clients who had also attended Eton, including Hugh and Gavin Astor, Lord Beit, Lord Carnarvon, M.A.R. and B. Cayzer, Lord Cholmondeley, Lord Drogheda, Lord Elgin, Abel-Smith, Lord Haddington, Lord Hambledon, Viscount Hindlip, the Duke of Westminster, Sacheverell Sitwell and Lord Rotherwick amongst others. These old friends, their colleagues and associates formed part of a social network through which Russell impressed and acquired more clients. It appears that Russell and Sunningdale had very little publicity to do as much of his promotion was by personal recommendation and by potential clients viewing his work first hand, either at the gardens and grounds of others or by visiting Sunningdale Nursery. The terms of address used in correspondence with Russell indicate the often friendly rather than business relationships he had with his clients, with, for example, the Marchioness of Dufferin and Ava nicknaming him 'Shrub'.

The number of people calling on Russell for advice, consultation and design escalated and much of his time was spent dashing around the country and over the Irish Sea, designing and planting, or otherwise entertaining people whilst they admired the nursery at Sunningdale, viewing plants which would form the landscapes created for them.

Expansion and the calls upon Russell resulting in time away from the nursery had the effect of Graham S. Thomas joining Sunningdale in 1956, taking a managerial roll for the next fifteen years. A number of letters written by G.S. Thomas relate to the rather 'big task of resuscitating this nursery',[4] possibly indicating that although Russell may have secured the horticultural standing of the business, with Sunningdale being revered as 'The most beautiful nursery', the financial side was rather unattractive. G.S. Thomas appears to have taken a firm stance on non-payment with

---

[2] From the presentation address by Professor Alistair Fitter on the occasion of the conferment of the honorary degree of Doctor of the University.
[3] JR/1/203.
[4] JR/1/329.

James Russell: Life and Works

several clients, such as Lady Rupert Nevill and Colonel K. Scheunert,[5] sending polite yet determined letters on the state of their accounts, and pursuing those defaulters who did not heed his correspondence, such as Randall Plunkett, with threats of legal action. Several appealed direct to Russell, indicative of the close relationships he enjoyed with his clients. It is apparent that a gentleman's agreement was often in place rather than a written business contract, with some clients paying for their projects in stages or even on an *ad hoc* basis.

Although many of the plants lists have prices it is quite rare to find any reference to the fees paid by clients for Russell's services. Very few of his clients inquired about his fees and there is equally little reference to such matters by Russell. However there are charges occasionally mentioned. For example between 1956 and 1985 the following daily fees were charged:

Year	Fee per day	File or client
1956	3 guineas	Stewart
1957	10 guineas	Stormont
1972	15 guineas	Thompson
1977	£60	Scott – Abu Dhabi
1985	£120	Rhododendrons - Wakehurst

Several files contain letters indicating confusion and shock over the bills sent to clients, many not realising that as well as being charged the fees for Russell's services, together with expenses, there would also be payment for any plan drawing, and that there would be packaging and posting charges on top of those for buying plants. By the time planting fees were added, which in 1971 were 15 guineas for Russell to place the plants, and possible charges for men to be brought from Sunningdale to do the labour if the client did not have staff, was unable to bring men in from outside or preferred to have all the work undertaken by Sunningdale Nurseries, the final cost could be significantly more than expected.

In 1968 Russell's personal connection with Sunningdale Nurseries came to an end as the business was sold to Waterers, following a disagreement with a cousin. Russell continued to work with Waterers in a

---

[5] JR/1/308 and JR/1/360.

consultancy role, but this was not always harmonious, with various negotiations about the business arrangements between the parties, and some conflict about how projects were run, including the billing of clients.

Castle Howard

Following his departure from Sunningdale Nurseries Russell moved to Castle Howard to become resident horticultural consultant for George Howard, Lord Howard of Henderskelfe, a close friend from his days at Eton. The majority of the large collection of rhododendrons at Sunningdale Nurseries was moved northwards and formed the basis for much of Russell's schemes. Although this had been agreed with Waterers, there was some contention about the exact number and type of plant that was being moved to Castle Howard, and up to a year later plants were still being lifted and transported.

Over the twenty-four years that Russell spent at Castle Howard several momentous projects were undertaken. In 1975 the Rose Garden was commissioned and Ray Wood, in which the rhododendron collection was planted out, was begun. Four years later, in 1979, the arboretum, 'perhaps his most striking achievement', was started.[6] In total the arboretum and Ray Wood encompasses over 130 acres and give some representation of Russell's lifelong enthusiasm for plants. Although keen for others to share his creation, his concern for the unique environment at Castle Howard is apparent. Several letters to estate staff, particularly to John Major, express his anxiety for the plants and annoyance with those visitors who did not heed notices.[7]

It was at Castle Howard that Russell furthered his interest in plants that required protection from the harsher elements of the British climate with the establishment of Exotic Plants and of a plant centre. Whilst at Sunningdale Nurseries Russell had designed several landscapes and planting plans for hot, temperate and cold houses, including at Abbots Ripton for Lord de Ramsey. Unfortunately circumstances went against such ventures, with oil prices rocketing in the 1970s, preventing many from

---

[6] From the presentation address by Professor Alistair Fitter on the occasion of the conferment of the honorary degree of Doctor of the University.
[7] JR/1/264.

heating their houses and prohibiting further expansion. However, Russell and the staff at Castle Howard did move towards a more modern style of marketing, despite his dislike of the garden centre. In 1980s Russell approached Marks & Spencer as a prospective retailer of plants but without success.[8]

The death of George Howard saw the end of the close connection of Russell with Castle Howard.

Work: Private and Commercial

Much of the landscape design undertaken by Russell whilst at Sunningdale was for private clients, with the scale of each project varying widely. Whereas for some Russell designed a border or bed, for others whole landscapes were planned. Russell was connected with some properties for a long period of time, either with an ongoing or consecutive project, or a short-term scheme, although these also ranged from an individual border to arboreta. There is one instance of Russell being called upon to redesign a garden that had fallen into disrepair some decades after he had originally created a landscape for it.[9]

Several of the gardens Russell was asked to work upon had an illustrious history, with, for example, Folly Farm, which was owned by Hugh Astor, being a Lutyens house with garden designed by Gertrude Jekyll. Another Lutyens and Jekyll property on which Russell worked was The Deanery, Sonning, for Nigel Broackes. Russell also landscaped part of Luton Hoo for Lady Wernher, the gardens designed by Capability Brown.

Russell believed that changes in taxation caused a down turn in the numbers of those who would call on his services as the properties he was usually called upon to landscape were 'the type of garden where you make a 20 year plan to include woods and the general landscape around the house'.[10] Although the large garden and grounds Russell was used to landscaping were in decline, his services were still called upon into the 1980s, with a garden in Normandy being designed for Lady Wimborne.

---

[8] JR/1/328.
[9] JR/1/229 and JR/1/44 for files relating to Fisherton Delamere House.
[10] From brief autobiography/resume of career by James Russell written for the Mount Agaki, Japan project.

James Russell: Life and Works

It appears that the landscaping of private gardens was, in part, responsible for the move to commercial work by Russell, with for example, Sir Edward Thompson being connected with the Redditch Development Corporation. Landscaping for business appears to have occurred, for the most part, following Russell's departure from Sunningdale Nurseries. Russell did quite a lot of work for Arup Associates, with other projects including landscape gardening for Lloyds Bank, Trebor and, perhaps most famously, for Wiggins Teape, with his creation being hailed as 'The Hanging Gardens of Basingstoke'.[11] The head office of General Accident at Pitheavlis was another commercial client, with Russell landscaping the interior and exterior of the complex. In comparison with his polite, peaceful and frequently friendly relationships with his private clients, those with his commercial clients were more distant. Russell sometimes battled to secure his designs and their implementation and often expressed exasperation at the lack of horticultural knowledge displayed by his clients. Indeed, there are instances where Russell firmly stands his ground, to the point of suggesting that unless an agreement is reached, whereby his advice is followed, his services will be withdrawn.

Later Work

Perhaps the largest project undertaken by Russell, and one of the last in his long career, was the landscaping of Mount Agaki, Japan, for the Seiyo Corporation. Russell had an advisory role in this project, which involved visits to Japan and a large amount of correspondence with individuals of the Seiyo Corporation and at the Botanic Gardens at Mount Agaki. This important project was covered in several copies of the newsletter of the Royal Horticultural Society of Japan.

Publications

Although a prolific landscape designer, plantsman and collector, in comparison with some of his contemporaries, such as Graham S. Thomas, Russell produced little literary work, representing his more hands on approach to gardening. He did, however, write several magazine articles

---

[11] See 'The Hanging Gardens of Basingstoke' by James Russell in *Interiors*, March 1984.

JAMES RUSSELL: LIFE AND WORKS

about his designs, and in particular the garden room he created at Castle Howard. These include 'The Dairies Castle Howard' by James Russell, in *Interiors* (June 1983), and 'James Russell' in 'The English Garden Room', edited by E. Dickinson (November 1986).

In 1962 Russell became involved with the Shell Gardens Scheme, possibly because of his connections with George Rainbird, book designer and publisher. Russell carefully thought about and created a list of gardens suitable for inclusion in a 'Shell Guide to English Gardens', and personally contacted the proprietors or estate staff. The project exemplifies the care and attention to detail shown by Russell in his work, as well as the high regard in which he was held.

Although Russell did not make a show of his work or court publicity, when exasperated stating that he was 'simply a gardener', his talents and vast knowledge were readily recognised. Many fellow horticulturalists consulted him about rhododendrons, roses and other plants, with, for example, members of the International Dendrology Society corresponding with him, and Desmond Clarke calling upon Russell's expertise when writing the supplement to W J Bean *The Trees and Shrubs Hardy in the British Isles*. He was also called upon to give lectures, including at Jodrell Bank Arboretum and to the Gardening Club at General Accident Head Office.

Travel

Although the majority of gardens Russell designed were in the United Kingdom, he did also work overseas. The gardens at Nassau, the Bahamas, for Sir Nicholas Nuttall are the most remote of all those gardens designed and the opportunity to work in this exotic climate appears to have been relished by Russell. Other gardens and landscaping were located on the Continent, such as the property in Normandy owned by Lady Wimborne and that in Monte Carlo by Sir Charles Clore, for which Russell designed a roof garden. Most of Russell's travelling, however, related to plant hunting expeditions (he was one of the first westerners to visit the People's Republic of China) and horticultural excursions. These included visits to America (1967), Madagascar (1979), Nassau, Georgia, Bahamas, Martinique, France (1980), Nassau, Sri Lanka (1981), Mexico, Nassau, France (1983), Mexico (1984), China (1985), Nassau (1986), Germany,

JAMES RUSSELL: LIFE AND WORKS

Austria, Japan (1987), Japan (1989), France, Japan (1990), as well as St. Lucia, Belgium and Holland.

Recognition

James Russell was not a person who relished publicity, although he did give an interview to the BBC, preferring to remain out of the spotlight. The nature of the work he undertook, being predominantly for private properties, has also led to very little being known about his work in comparison with others. There is, however, occasional reference to his landscaping in promotional literature provided for gardens with which he was involved, such as at Glenveagh Park, the gardens of which Henry P. McIlhenny developed 'with his advisors Jim Russell and Lanning Roper'[12] and at the Secret Garden at Highclere Castle 'where the curving herbaceous beds and serpentine paths were designed for the present Earl's father by James Russell'.[13]

Although the majority of Russell's work was in the creation of private gardens, it is for his designs for commercial clients that Russell is perhaps best known. His landscape design for Wiggins Teape won a certificate of commendation from the Civic Trust Award in 1978. Other work, which may have received wider public attention, was the various garden designs created for the Ideal Homes Exhibitions of 1963, 1974 and 1975, but perhaps if it hadn't been for his connection with Lord Rothermere, this opportunity may never have presented itself.

The Royal Horticultural Society, from whom he received the Veitch Memorial Award and the Society's highest award, the Victoria Medal of Honour, has also applauded Russell's horticultural knowledge and landscape design expertise. The University of York is another organisation that has acknowledged the merits of Russell, awarding him an honorary degree of Doctor of the University in 1994 in recognition of his contribution to botany and conservation. Russell's involvement with the Hillier Arboretum, from its transition into public ownership until the 1980s, both on the Management Committee and the Standing Advisory Panel, indicates the high regard in which he was held throughout the horticultural world. Together with institutions many individuals have shown recognition of his

---
[12] http://homepage.tinet.ie/~dmcfadden/page11/html, 14 March 2002
[13] http://www.higclerecastle.co.uk/w-gardens.htm, 9 October 2001

JAMES RUSSELL: LIFE AND WORKS

skill and knowledge, praising him as 'one of Britain's greatest modern plantsmen'[14] and as one of the 'most influential landscape gardeners in the world'.[15]

James Russell died on 28 April 1996, aged 76.

---

[14] Lin Hawthorne, horticulturalist, in 'The Castle Howard Collection', *The Garden*, Oct. 1997, pp. 742-747, at p. 742.
[15] In correspondence to James Russell from Laura Ponsonby, March 1989.

JAMES RUSSELL ARCHIVE: ADMINISTRATIVE HISTORY

Provenance and Arrangement

Before the deposit of the archive in the University of York the papers appear to have been kept with James Russell, rather than being permanently lodged with the business he was involved with. Many files relate to landscapes designed whilst Russell was connected with Sunningdale Nurseries, which he left following its acquisition by Waterers in 1968 (itself acquired by Northcutts Nurseries in 1982), and with Exotic Plants, Castle Howard. Following his departure from Castle Howard, the paperwork appears to have been kept at his other residences, with papers being shipped to the University of York from Scotland in a trunk.

Russell deposited the papers before his retirement, via the Garden History Society through the intervention of Peter Goodchild of the Institute of Advanced Architectural Studies, the University of York. The archive was deposited at the Borthwick Institute of Historical Research, University of York in June 1995, after being housed at the Institute of Advanced Architectural Studies, University of York since 1993. Further additions were made to the archive in October 1996, June 1997 and June 1999.

The files have been retained in the order used by James Russell by client, which was an approximation towards alphabetical sequence, with those names, such as Van Oss or De Ramsey being filed under the first part of the name, i.e. Van or De. The files include correspondence and some folded plans. Where plans were too large to fit into the filing system Russell stored them as separate rolls. These were also arranged alphabetically. In general the files and plans relating to one client share the same title, although there are exceptions. For instance the file relating to designs for Culzean Castle, is titled 'Culzean' while the plans are headed 'National Trust of Scotland', and the file for the scheme at Cholmondeley Castle is headed 'Cholmondeley' and the plans are labelled 'Rocksavage', indicating the change in title of the proprietor. Another example of some confusion as to the title of a project is with work carried out for Nigel Broackes at Hyde Park Gate, with the file being placed with other Broackes material, but the plans were rolled in the bundle labelled 'H'. Ordnance

James Russell Archive: Administrative History

survey maps were, with the odd exception, kept separately from the planting plans and files. In those instances where the client has not been named the file or plans have been placed under the name of the property.

Papers within the files are arranged in reverse chronological order. Plans were frequently separated from correspondence and other paperwork, but these have now been collectively placed in folders.

The majority of files are composed of correspondence, both letters received and sent by Russell. Russell's letters can contain just a short expression of his ideas for a garden, or a long and in depth report. Plant lists, often marked with prices, frequently accompany these. More mundane administrative paperwork appears to have been issued by others, with Sunningdale Nurseries responsible for much of this work in the earlier part of his career. Planting plans are also included in many of the files, occasionally with the original draft made by Russell.

Other documents which occur in the files include quotations, invoices, orders, confirmation and delivery notes, import and export licences and other official documentation, photographs, and on the odd occasion, a dried leaf or flower.

Together with the files Russell deposited photocopies of twenty-two pages of notes. These contain his knowledge about the current ownership of the properties, such as whether the client is deceased, the condition of the gardens, often lamenting deterioration, ruin or vandalism in the case of public parks, whether work was carried out or if it only reached the planning stage. Sometimes Russell gives the reason for non completion, such as the sale of the property, or, in the case of the Duke and Duchess of Northumberland, that 'it is either the garden or your hunting!' (said the Duke to the Duchess), and other notes of interest. Russell also states which files he thinks would not be of interest to York, which files that should stay at Castle Howard or not enter the public domain, and other files that have been lost over time. Russell kept files and plans of those gardens for which work was not eventually carried out, including, for example Mrs Abel-Smith, Lord Abergavenny, Mr Galliers-Pratt, Baron Guy de Rothschild, Lady Richard Percy.

In the majority of files plans have been kept with the correspondence. These plans are, normally, dyeline, are frequently annotated, and occasionally muddy and torn, very much showing Russell's

James Russell Archive: Administrative History

active process when designing a garden. The master copies of plans were kept separately, in rolls, interleaved with headed brown paper identifying each client, although this does not appear to been consistently employed. The ordnance survey maps, which accompany some of the larger gardens and grounds that Russell worked on, were also been kept separately, with infrequent reference to which client the map belongs.

Physical Condition, Conservation and Preservation

The conditions in which the documents were kept appear to have left a little to be desired, with several plans suffering from rodent abuse and others being damaged by water and other liquids. Documents have also been damaged by the use of steel paper clips, pins and various sticky tapes to fasten documents. Photostat copies of documents and faxes have been recopied onto permasafe paper in order to prevent further deterioration.

Potential Use of the Archive

As well as providing material for the history of gardening the James Russell Archive provides an insight into far more, with much of the correspondence providing a social, political and economic commentary on the second half of the twentieth century.

The files provide a wealth of information about individual properties. Later notes by Russell contain details of the then present state of gardens he worked on, stating if they had been sold or altered, whether they had fallen into disrepair or suffered from vandalism, such as at the Holt Memorial Garden, Birkenhead, and the Redditch Development Corporation. The files show the perpetual development of gardens, with Russell making his mark upon gardens designed and landscaped by Gertrude Jekyll and Capability Brown. The files also give present day owners of those gardens that Russell designed the information they need to maintain or reinstate his original planting schemes.

Although a large proportion of the designing undertaken by Russell was for private clients, he did landscape several commercial

James Russell Archive: Administrative History

properties. The files give some insight into the history of landscape design in a commercial sense and of building beautification; something appreciated by those who worked in an otherwise sterile environment. The award given for the landscape at Wiggins Teape, Basingstoke, demonstrates the growing recognition of the importance of a high-quality working environment.

The archive gives some indication of the development of garden design and landscaping. The Ideal Homes exhibition is one example of the participation by Russell in a more commercial setting, using the event to showcase his work to a far wider audience than would normally have been available. This public display is quite a contrast to the normal route by which people came to see Russell's work, which was, for the most part, by word of mouth or by visiting other people's gardens or Sunningdale Nurseries, and subsequently inviting him to design their own garden or grounds.

Russell's visit to China is striking in that he was one of first westerners to travel there following the revolution. The correspondence gives a wonderful insight into not only the exploits of plant hunting and other associated disciplines, but also of the intricate arrangements necessary for such an enterprise. China is a perfect illustration of Russell's determination to seize an opportunity as it presented itself, as is his involvement with a project for Government Centre, Mauritius: 'I don't think anything actually happened (I was hoping to go out & do some interesting collecting on the side)'.

As well as providing information about the plant collecting performed by Russell in person, the archive gives details of his subscription to other people's collecting expeditions, such as that led by Chris Chadwell to Kashmir and Fergus Kinmouth to Bhutan, and the closely knit horticultural world. This later point is strengthened by frequent mention of individuals sending one another a cutting of this or a seed of that, giving evidence of how various plants entered the country and found their way into numerous gardens. The archive provides a wealth of information about rhododendrons in the United Kingdom and other parts of the world, with, for example, a large part of the famed collection of rhododendrons at Sunningdale moving with Russell to Castle Howard to form Ray Wood.

James Russell Archive: Administrative History

The archive provides great detail for the study of nurseries and garden centres, particularly of the movement away from specialist nurseries towards more general garden centres. This in turn gives some indication of a change in the type of customer using these enterprises, and their number, with the reduction in size of many of the larger gardens and parks, for a variety of reasons, and the growth of interest in gardens by the public at large, and the willingness or capacity to spend upon them.

Reference to the high costs of maintaining greenhouses, gardens and parks is found in several of the files. Several of the properties mentioned, including the Hillier Arboretum, the Isle of Gigha and Hare Hill, were given to trusts, while Lord de Ramsey frequently complains of the high cost involved in running the tropical houses at Abbots Ripton. The difficulty in finding good gardeners, even for those gardens with a national reputation, also presents itself, with many clients requesting landscapes that don't need constant attention and asking Russell to recommend suitable individuals.

The close ties between many of Russell's clients are also identifiable, with, for example, many of them having attended Eton (indeed, his old school also had gardens designed by him). These school friendships and associations appear to have lead to other individuals requesting Russell's services, mostly for their own properties, but sometimes for associated companies. For example, both Russell and Lord Rothermere attended Eton, possibly creating the opportunity for Russell to present his designs at the Ideal Home Exhibition, with which Lord Rothermere was connected by his position with the Daily Mail newspaper, as well as at his private residence. Patronage, and the importance of connections, is also apparent with Loelia, Duchess of Westminster, for whom Russell created plans for her residence at The Old Vicarage, Send, as well as for the Yvonne Arnaud Theatre of which she was a patron.

JAMES RUSSELL ARCHIVE: ACCESS

Access

Jim Russell's wishes, when he gave his papers to the Garden History Society, were that his papers should benefit students and scholars. It is in this spirit that the James Russell Archive is made available at the Borthwick Institute. There are, however, legal considerations in granting access to the archive that did not pertain during Russell's lifetime. Because the papers are so recent, and relate in many cases to living individuals, the provisions of the Data Protection Act 1998 apply to the archive. In essence this means that scholars may access the papers only after agreeing to comply with the provisions of the Act in relation to the research exemption. These provisions are that:

i. research will not be used to support measures or decisions with respect to particular individuals;
ii. research will not cause or be likely to cause substantial damage or substantial distress to any person who is the subject of those data while he or she is alive (assuming a life span of 100 years);
iii. the results of research shall not be made available in a form which identifies any data subject without the consent in writing of the data subject and the data controller.

In addition to these legal requirements, the Borthwick wishes to ensure that researchers respect the privacy of the present owners of the gardens documented in Russell's plans.

Access to the Russell Archive is therefore granted on the following conditions:

i. Researchers must sign an agreement acknowledging that they understand their obligations under the Data Protection Act.
ii. Citation, quotation or reproduction of the papers must not identify extant gardens that are not accessible to the public, except with the written permission of the garden owner, a copy of which permission must be given to the Borthwick Institute in advance of any such citation, quotation or reproduction.

JR   # JAMES RUSSELL ARCHIVE

James Russell, landscape gardener and nurseryman, 1920-1996

JR/1   CLIENTS' FILES

JR/1/1   Abel-Smith, Mrs
Houndsell Place, Mark Cross, Crowborough, Sussex
1954-1958
Correspondence with plant list and planting plans for borders and garden.
1 file; 1 roll

JR/1/2   Aberconway, Lady
Maenan Hall, Llanrwst, North Wales   1961-1965
Correspondence with plant list and planting plan for borders and rose groups.
1 file

JR/1/3   Abergavenny, Marquis of
Eridge Castle, Tunbridge Wells, Kent   1954
Correspondence with plant list and planting plans for borders and garden.
1 file; 1 roll

JR/1/4   Adair, Major General Sir A. Bt.
Holy Hill, Strabane, co. Tyrone, Northern Ireland
1957-1959
Correspondence, Ordnance Survey map, plant lists and planting plans for borders and garden.
1 file; 1 roll

JR/1/5   Airlie, Earl and Countess of
Airlie Castle, Craigton, Angus, Scotland and Cortachy Castle, Kirriemuir, Angus, Scotland   1954-1958
Correspondence, also with Mr. Paton and Mr. Wardhaugh, Ordnance Survey maps, plant lists and planting plans for rhododendron groups and garden.
1 file; 1 roll

James Russell Archive

JR/1/6   **Alston, N.**
         Green Farm, East Tuddenham, Dereham, Norfolk   1983-1984
         Correspondence with planting plan for garden.
         1 file; 1 roll

JR/1/7   **Anson, Mrs G.H.**
         Calton Hall, Burton-upon-Trent, Staffordshire   1962-1966
         Correspondence, also with Sunningdale Nurseries, with invoices, plant lists and planting plans for garden.
         1 file; 1 roll

JR/1/8   **Arboretum des Barres, France**   1983
         Correspondence; 'Catalogue des Graines', 1983-1985; notes in French 'Le Domaine des Barres'; Notes on the Arboretum of Les Barres with plan, September 1983; Notes on the Arboretum of Balaine, France, October 1966.
         1 file

JR/1/9   **Arthur, Mrs E.**
         Longnor Hall, near Shrewsbury, Shropshire   1952-1963
         Correspondence, also with Mr. G.S. Thomas and Sunningdale Nurseries, plant lists and planting plans for garden (original file marked 'main plans missing').
         1 file; 1 roll

JR/1/10 **Ashbrook, Viscountess**
         Arley Hall, Northwich, Cheshire   1964-1966
         Correspondence, Ordnance Survey map, plant lists and planting plans for gardens in the chapel ground, 'The Rootery', the walled garden and 'The Rough'.
         1 file; 2 rolls

JR/1/11 **Askew, Mr. G.**
         Bentley Farm, Halland, Lewes, Sussex   1961-1963
         Ordnance Survey maps, planting plans and sketches for rose borders, white garden, goose field, the sloping garden and the garden.
         see also JR/1/13
         1 file; 2 rolls

James Russell Archive

JR/1/12　***Askew, Mr. I.***
Wellingham House, Lewes, Sussex　　　1962-1972
Correspondence, plant list and planting plans for the garden.
1 file; 2 rolls

JR/1/13　***Askew, Mrs. M.***
Bentley Farm, Halland, Lewes, Sussex　　　1982-1984
Correspondence, including correspondence with P.G. Zwijnenberg, The Netherlands, invoices, plant lists and planting plans for a formal garden. Also contains a booklet: 'Bentley', (East Sussex County Council, April 1982), with the history of the family and property, and information about Wildfowl Reserve and Motor Museum.
see also, JR/1/11
1 file; 2 rolls

JR/1/14　***Ascot Racecourse, Berkshire***　　　1954-1955
Planting plans for new paddock.
1 file; 2 rolls

JR/1/15　***Astor, The Hon. G. and Lady I.***
Hever Castle, Edenbridge, Kent; Tillypronie, Tarland, Aberdeenshire; and Wickenden Manor, Sharpthorne, Sussex　　　1960-1965
Correspondence, also with Sunningdale Nurseries and gardeners, together with plant lists and planting plans for rose borders, pink borders, herb garden at Hever Castle and gardens at both properties.
1 file; 2 rolls

JR/1/16　***Astor, the Hon. Lt. Col. H and Mrs E.***
Folly Farm, Sulhamstead, Berkshire　　　1955-1957
Correspondence, including with Sunningdale Nurseries and Mr. Jones, plant lists and planting plans for borders and garden.
1 file; 2 rolls

JR/1/17　***Attwood, Mrs. A.***
Ruckley Grange, Shifnal, Shropshire; Trefri Lodge, Aberdovey, Merionethshire　　　1964-1965
Correspondence with plant lists and planting plan for rose border and garden.
1 file; 2 rolls

JAMES RUSSELL ARCHIVE

JR/1/18 ***Arup Associates: Wiggins Teape Ltd., Gateway House, Basingstoke, Hampshire***   1973-1981
Correspondence, memoranda, plant lists, building and planting plans for roof gardens: terraces and courtyards, and grounds, reports, orders and invoices, minutes and a certificate of commendation from the Civic Trust Awards, 1978, relating to the design and creation of roof gardens and other landscaping. Individuals, businesses and organisations involved include Civic Trust, N. Cowell of the Polytechnic of the South Bank, Lindsey Pirrie and John Buchanan of Wiggins Teape, Charles Funke of Craigwell Nurseries and Flower House Display Ltd., L.A. Stockwell of Exbury Gardens Ltd., and K.G. Illett of Bovis Construction.
1 file

JR/1/19 ***Arup Associates: IBM, Havant, Hampshire***   1978-1980
Correspondence, invoices, plant lists, memoranda and planting plans for courtyards and grounds at IBM, Havant. Individuals, businesses and organisations involved include Stapeley Water Gardens Ltd., P.M. Fryer of Messrs. Pearson & Ward, solicitors, Mr. K.G. Illett and Charles Funke of Craigwell Nurseries.
1 file

JR/1/20 ***Arup Associates: H.M. Naval Base Portsmouth, Extension Area, Hampshire***   1975-1979
Correspondence, plant lists, and building and planting plans for courtyards and grounds. Individuals, businesses and organisations involved include W.E. Chivers & Sons Ltd., and A.P. Dunball of the Department of Transport.
1 file

JR/1/21 ***Arup Associates: Dammam Social Insurance, Saudi Arabia***   1978
Correspondence, plant lists and building and planting plans.
1 file

JR/1/22 ***Arup Associates: Lloyd's, Chatham, Kent***   1977-1979
Correspondence, invoices, plant lists, building and planting plans for courtyard and grounds.
1 file

JAMES RUSSELL ARCHIVE

JR/1/23 **Arup Associates: IBM, North Harbour, Portsmouth, Hampshire**
1978-1981
Correspondence, plant lists, invoices and building and planting plans for courtyards, terraces, roof gardens and grounds.
1 file; 1 roll

JR/1/24 **Arup Associates: Trebor, Colchester factory, Essex**
1978-1979
Correspondence, minutes, memoranda, plant lists, planting plans for courtyards and grounds. Individuals, businesses and organisations involved include L.A. Stockwell of Exbury Trees, K. Illett of Craigwell Nurseries, T. Drew of Exbury Gardens. Also contains a catalogue of Bernhard's Rugby Nurseries Ltd.
1 file

JR/1/25 **Ascott, Wing, Leighton Buzzard, Bedfordshire**   1983-1987
Correspondence with John Sales of the National Trust, Evelyn de Rothschild, Victoria de Rothschild, Julian and John Prideaux and others, catalogue for Civic Trees 1984-5, soil analysis, Ordnance Survey maps, plant lists and planting plans for fern garden, Hidcote garden, Dutch garden, Madeira walk and grounds.
1 file; 2 rolls

JR/1/26 **Bagrit, Sir Leon**
Ascot Place, Ascot, Berkshire   1967
Plant list from Sunningdale Nurseries.
1 file

JR/1/27 **Baillie, Major S.**
Harleyburn, Melrose, Roxburghshire and Allanbank, Lauder, Berwickshire, Scotland   1965-1974
Correspondence, plant lists and planting plans for gardens.
1 file; 1 roll

JR/1/28 **Bainbridge, G.V.M.**
Roecliff Lodge   nd 1950s
Planting plans for heather garden, borders and garden.
1 file

James Russell Archive

JR/1/29 *Baker-Wilbraham, Lady*
Rode Hall, Scholar Green, Cheshire   1962-1966
Correspondence, Ordnance Survey map, plant list and planting plans for garden.
1 file; 1 roll

JR/1/30 *Ballard, Helen*
Old Country, Mathon, Malvern, Worcestershire   1980
Correspondence and catalogue of snowdrops: 'List No. 110'.
1 file

JR/1/31 *Barker, Capt. F.G.*
Lushill House, Highworth, Wiltshire   1966-1984
Correspondence, quotations for glasshouses, sketches, plant list, and planting plans for borders and garden.
1 file; 1 roll

JR/1/32 *Beckwith Smith, Mrs*
The Old Rectory, Sullinstead, near Newbury, Berkshire
                                                       1959-1970
Correspondence and plant lists.
1 file; 1 roll

JR/1/33 *Behrens, Col. W.*
Swinton Grange, Malton, Yorkshire   1954-1966
Correspondence, also with Sunningdale Nurseries, plant lists and planting plans for terraces, borders and garden.
1 file; 1 roll

JR/1/34 *Behrens, Mr Michael and Mrs Felicity*
Culham Court, Berkshire   1961-1964
Correspondence, also with H.C. Aubrey & Sons, Reading, Ordnance Survey maps, plant lists and planting plans for caravan site, walled garden, swimming pool and garden.
1 file; 1 roll

JAMES RUSSELL ARCHIVE

JR/1/35 **Beit, Lord and Lady**
Russborough, Blessington, Co. Wicklow, Eire 1953-1985
Correspondence, also with Thomas Rochford & Sons Ltd, Turnford Hall Nurseries, Sir Martyn Beckett, Caulfields Ltd. and others, including telegrams, invoices, Ordnance Survey maps, plant lists, sketches of views and building and planting plans for aviary, walled garden, herbaceous border, garden
1 file; 1 roll; 1 plan folder

JR/1/36 **Bell MacDonald, Mr. A.M.**
Rammerscales, Lockerbie, Dumfrieshire, Scotland 1968-1970
Correspondence, plant list and planting plan for border.
1 file

JR/1/37 **Bernhard's Nursery, Bilton Road, Rugby, Warwickshire**
1978-1979
Correspondence and 'Nursery Stock Availability List, January 1979'
1 file

JR/1/38 **Berry, Lady Pamela**
Oving House, Whitchurch, Aylesbury, Buckinghamshire 1955-1957
Correspondence, sketches, Ordnance Survey map, plant lists and planting plan for borders and garden.
1 file; 1 roll

JR/1/39 **Bertie, Peregrine**
Brockdale House, Warfield, Berkshire 1967-1969
Correspondence, plant lists and planting plans for borders and garden.
1 file; 1 roll

JR/1/40 **Birdlands Zoo, Bourton-on-the-water, Gloucestershire**
1967
Correspondence, plant list and planting plan for Flamingo Canal.
1 file; 1 roll

JR/1/41 **Birley, Lady Rhoda**
Charleston Manor, West Dean, Seaford, Sussex 1965-1972
Correspondence, also with Chris Brickell, John Mattock and Patrick M. Synge, primarily about roses.
1 file

JAMES RUSSELL ARCHIVE

JR/1/42 *Stewart-Black, Major I. Hervey*
Little Dunbarnie, Bridge of Earn, Perth; Old Manse, Balfron, Stirlingshire   1954-1984
Correspondence, also to John Waterer Sons & Crisp Ltd, plant lists and planting plans for garden.
1 file

JR/1/43 *Mairs, Col. A.*
Chiltern Park, Kalorama, Victoria, Australia   1980-1984
Correspondence.
1 file

JR/1/44 *Blake-Tyler, Mrs. Rosemary*
Fisherton Delamere House, Wylye, Wiltshire   1958-1959
Correspondence, plant list and planting plans.
See also JR/1/229
1 file

JR/1/45 **Blackpool Tower, Lancashire**   1976-1978
Correspondence, also with OAD Agriculture Ltd. and Craigwell Nurseries, an article from 'Turnstone's Sportsman's Diary', plant lists, and planting plans for butterfly exhibition, monkey jungle and tropical jungle free flight aviary.
1 file

JR/1/46 *Blyth, Betty*
Melgund Glen, Minto, Hawick, Roxburghshire   1966
Correspondence, plant list, Ordnance Survey map and planting plans for grounds.
1 file; 1 roll

JR/1/47 **M. Bonham-Carter**
42 Victoria Road, London   1955
Sketch of garden and planting plans for garden.
1 file; 1 roll

JAMES RUSSELL ARCHIVE

JR/1/48 **Bostock, Mr G. and Mrs D.**
Tixall Cottage, Tixall, Staffordshire   1958-1967
Correspondence, Ordnance Survey map, plant lists and planting plans for avenue and garden.
1 file; 1 roll

JR/1/49 **Broackes, Nigel, Mortimer House**   1970-1971
Correspondence, plant lists, sketches and planting plans for swimming pool.
1 file

JR/1/50 **Broackes, Nigel, 52-54 Hyde Park Gate, London**
                                                       1966-1967
Correspondence, minutes, plant list and building and planting plans for garden.
1 file; 1 roll

JR/1/51 **Broackes, Nigel**
La Bastide de la Roquette, Cannes, France   1977-1978
Correspondence, plant lists, maps and planting plans for garden.
1 file

JR/1/52 **Broackes, Nigel**
21 Chelsea Square, London   1977
Correspondence with Sunningdale Nurseries, plant list and planting plan for garden.
1 file

JR/1/53 **Broackes, Nigel**
The Deanery, Sonning, Berkshire   1974-1976
Correspondence, also to Chapman Taylor Partners, notes of site visits, plant lists, sketches and planting plans for swimming pool, borders and garden.
1 file

JR/1/54 **Broackes, Nigel**
Wargrave Manor, Wargrave, Berkshire   1966-1973
Correspondence, also with Chapman Tayor Partners, Bridge Walker Ltd., John Waterer Sons & Crisp Ltd., Thomas Rivers & Son Ltd., V.

JAMES RUSSELL ARCHIVE

Russell Smith and others, minutes of site meetings, invoices, notes on Paul Jones paintings, notes on plants, plant lists, and building and planting plans for pool pavillion, rose beds, orchard, greenhouses, garden and grounds.
1 file; 1 roll

JR/1/55 **Bowers, Mrs**
No address given 1960
Report on garden and plant list.
1 file

JR/1/56 **Bourke-Borrowes, K.H.**
Sissinghurst Castle, Kent 1971-1975
Correspondence.
1 file

JR/1/57 **Boyle, Lady Nell, Capt. M.P.R.**
Ashe Park, near Basingstoke, Hampshire 1963-1964
Correspondence, Ordnance Survey map, quotations, plant list and planting plans for garden.
1 file; 1 roll

JR/1/58 **Bradford Estate Forestry Department**
The Bungalow, Weston-under-Lizard, Shifnal, Staffordshire
1977-1979
Correspondence.
1 file

JR/1/59 **Bradstock, Mrs**
Clanville Lodge, Clanville, Andover, Hampshire 1969
Correspondence, plant list, Ordnance Survey map and planting plan for beds.
1 file

JR/1/60 **Brent Cross Shopping Centre, London** 1977
Correspondence with C.D. Brickell and Donaldson & Sons.
1 file

James Russell Archive

JR/1/61 **Bristol, Clifton and West of England Zoological Society**
Bristol, Avon 1978-1984
Correspondence, plant lists, orders and delivery notes.
1 file

JR/1/62 **Brockway, M.**
New Place, Farmington, Cheltenham, Gloucestershire
1967-1970
Correspondence, plant list, sketch and building and planting plans for garden.
1 file

JR/1/63 **Brocklehurst, Col. C. and Mrs**
Hare Hill, Macclesfield, Cheshire 1960-1977
Correspondence, plant lists and planting plans for borders and garden.
1 file; 1 roll

JR/1/64 **Brompton Hospital Sanitorium, Frimley, Sussex** 1953-1965
Correspondence, also with Sunningdale Nurseries and Wealdon Woodlands Ltd., invoices, plant lists, planting plans for garden.
1 file

JR/1/65 **Bromley-Davenport, Col. Sir W.**
Capesthorne Hall, Macclesfield, Cheshire 1955-1970
Correspondence, also with G.S. Thomas and Sunningdale Nurseries, Ordnance Survey map, plant lists and planting plans for beds, borders and lake area.
1 file; 1 roll

JR/1/66 **Brooke, Humphrey**
8 Pelham Crescent, London 1974-1983
Correspondence about roses and list of Sangerhausen Roses at Scott's.
1 file

JR/1/67 **Brooking, Paul**
Neo Plants Ltd, 197 Kirkham Road, Freckelton, Lancashire
1985
Correspondence and leaflet 'New Lines for Spring 1985'.
1 file

James Russell Archive

JR/1/68 **Bruce, Hon. James**
Balmanno Castle, Perth, Scotland; and Dron House, Balmanno, Perthshire, Scotland 1963-1988
Correspondence, plant lists, Ordnance Survey map and planting plans for garden and grounds.
1 file; O/S map in roll

JR/1/69 **Balniel, Lord Robin**
107 Frognal, Hampstead, London 1973
Correspondence, plant list and planting plan for garden (originally part of Bruce file).
1 file

JR/1/70 **Brudenell, Hon. Mr Edmund and Mrs Marion**
Deene Park, Corby, Northamptonshire 1963-1971
Correspondence, soil analysis, Ordnance Survey map and planting plans for borders, the White Garden and garden and grounds.
1 file; 1 roll

JR/1/71 **Bryce, Mrs Ivor**
Moyns Park, Steeple Bumpstead, Haverhill, Suffolk 1956-1957
Correspondence also with Sunningdale Nurseries and Fisher, Dowson & Wasbrough.
1 file

JR/1/72 **Bowlby, The Hon. David and Mrs Penelope**
Inverinate, Kyles of Lochalsh, Wester Rosse, Scotland and The Manor, Healing, Grimsby, Lincolnshire 1952-1974
Correspondence, also with members of the estate at Inverinate, Sunningdale Nurseries, Fraser & Ross, and Stanley & Co., solicitors, plant lists, invoices, and planting plans for gardens. Also includes report of Sunningdale Nurseries, 'Position at End of 1964-5 Season'.
1 file; 1 roll; 1 plan folder

JR/1/73 **Burgett, Mr James and Mrs Sharon**
Ellens Green, Rudgwick, Sussex 1970
Correspondence, plant list and planting plan for garden.
1 file

James Russell Archive

JR/1/74 **Burnett of Leys, Jamie**
Castle Airy, Banochory, Kincardineshire, Scotland
                                                                    1975
Correspondence also with Fibrelite Engineering Ltd, and 2 samples of plastic.
1 file

JR/1/75 **Butler, Mr Richard and Mrs Susan**
Penny Pot, Halstead, Essex   1960-1962
Correspondence, plant list and planting plan for garden.
1 file; 1 roll

JR/1/76 **Butter, Mr David and Mrs Myra**
Eastwood, Dunkeld, Perthshire   1969-1971
Correspondence, plant list and planting plan for borders.
1 file

JR/1/77 **Buildings**   1961-1965
Correspondence with Louis Gray & Mutch, Mount Lodge, Station Parade, Sunningdale and with Maurice Mason and other individuals, quotations and catalogues from, correspondence with and orders to various businesses including Unique Dutch Light Co. Ltd, customs declaration forms, sketch of chair and orangery, promotional literature 'The Orangery - designed and planted by James Russell, The Sunningdale Nurseries'.
1 file

JR/1/78 **Calvocoressi, Mrs**
The Tor, South Ascot, Berkshire   1956
Planting plan for garden.
1 file; 1 roll

JR/1/79 **Cameron of Lochiel, Col. D.H. and Margaret**
Achnacarry, Spean Bridge, Inverness-shire, Scotland
                                                                    1954-1958
Correspondence, plant list and planting plan for grounds.
1 file

AMES RUSSELL ARCHIVE

JR/1/80 **Cameron, Mr. E.**
Terrington House, Terrington, Yorkshire   1974
Correspondence, plant list and planting plan for garden.
1 file

JR/1/81 **Camu, Mme Theresa and Alain**
55 Dreve des Gendarmes, Brussels, Belgium   1966
Correspondence, plant list and planting plan for gardens.
1 file; 1 roll

JR/1/82 **Carnarvon, Earls of**
Milford Lake House, Burghclere, Newbury, Berkshire, and Highclere Castle, near Newbury, Berkshire   1962-1991
Correspondence, also with Doug. Harris of Penwood Nurseries, Penwood, and other nurseries, orders and invoices, sketches, schedules of planting, plant lists, Ordnance Survey map and planting plans for Temple area, the glade, walled garden, gardens and grounds.
1 file; 1 roll

JR/1/83 **Cayzer, The Hon. M.A.R.**
Great Westwood, King's Langley, Hertsfordshire; 2 Ilchester Place, London, and Walhurst Manor, Cowfold, Sussex
     1967-1989
Correspondence, Ordnance Survey map, plant lists and planting plans for rose garden, border and gardens.
see also JR/1/350
1 file; 2 rolls

JR/1/84 **Cayzer, Bernard**
Parish's, Timsbury, Somerset, and Cayzer House, 2 & 4 St Mary Axe, London   1954-1966
Correspondence, also with Colefax & Fowler Associates Ltd. and Sunningdale Nurseries, plant lists, sketches and building and planting plans for roof garden, border, rose garden and garden.
1 file; 1 roll

JAMES RUSSELL ARCHIVE

JR/1/85 ***The Country Gentlemen's Association Ltd***
Trading Division, Icknield Way West, Letchworth, Hertfordshire
1973, 1980

Correspondence.
1 file

JR/1/86 ***Chapman, A.C.B.***
Kent House, Keswick Road, Cringleford, Norwich, Norfolk
1969

Correspondence, plant list, section of Ordnance Survey and planting plans for garden.
1 file

JR/1/87 ***Chapman, Robert and Virginia***
Debden Manor, Saffron Walden, Essex *1975-1976*
Correspondence, plant lists and planting plans for gardens.
1 file

JR/1/88 ***Charterhouse***
Godalming, Surrey *1974-1976*
Correspondence, also with Charterhouse, London, plant lists and planting plans for garden.
1 file

JR/1/89 ***Chateris, Virginia***
The Grange, Elvington, Yorkshire *1972-1973*
Correspondence and plant lists.
1 file

JR/1/90 ***Chatto, Beth .***
Unusual Plants, White Barn House, Elmstead Market, Colchester, Essex *1988-1990*
Correspondence and order.
1 file

JR/1/91 ***Chilstone (Garden Ornaments)***
Great Linford Manor, Newport Pagnell, Buckinghamshire
1973

Correspondence.
1 file

James Russell Archive

JR/1/92 **Cholmondeley, Marquess and Marchioness of**
Cholmondeley Castle, Malpas, Cheshire   1960-1985
Correspondence, plant lists and planting plans for pool garden, gardens and grounds.
1 file; 1 roll

JR/1/93 **Clarke, Desmond**
Chase Cottage, Chase Lane, Haslemere, Surrey   1982-1988
Correspondence and plant notes.
1 file

JR/1/94 **Clarke, Mrs Patsy**
Loughbrow House, Hexham, Northumberland   1962-1966
Correspondence, planting lists and planting plans for shrub border, woodland and garden at Mount Armstrong.
1 file

JR/1/95 **Clifton Nurseries Ltd, Garden Centres**
Clifton Vill, London   1979-1980
Correspondence with Mrs. Honan of Clifton Nurseries Ltd, the Earl of Drogheda and the Hon. J. Rothschild.
1 file

JR/1/96 **Clive, Brig. A.F.L.**
Perrystone Court, Ross, Herefordshire   1960-1963
Correspondence, plant lists, section of Ordnance Survey map and building and planting plans for garden.
1 file; 1 roll

JR/1/97 **Clore, Sir Charles**
Les Floriales, Av. Britanique, Monte Carlo   1979
Correspondence, quotations, contracts, list of contractors, and planting plans for roof garden.
1 file; 1 roll

JR/1/98 **Cochran-Patrick, Neil**
Auchenham, Beith, Ayrshire   nd 1950s?
Planting plans for border and garden.
1 file; 1 roll

JAMES RUSSELL ARCHIVE

JR/1/99   *Coke, Viscount*
          Holkham Hall, Wells-next-the-sea, Norfolk   1988-1991
          Correspondence, also with nurseries, orders and invoices, plant lists, maps and planting plans for rose garden, garden and parterre, with plans for parterre from 1853.
          1 file

JR/1/100 *Collin, Lady Clarissa*
          Wytherstone House, Pockley, Yorkshire   1976
          Correspondence re. sale of statues, also with Boulton & Cooper Ltd.
          1 file

JR/1/101 *Colvin, Mrs*
          Peacock Hills, Woldringford, Horsham, Sussex and Old Woldringford, Horsham, Surrey   1962-1966
          Correspondence, plant list and planting plan for Pond Garden.
          1 file; 1 roll

JR/1/102 *Connell, Lady Audrey*
          Colquhalzie, Auchterarder, Perthshire, Scotland
          1964-1972
          Correspondence, also with Sunningdale Nurseries, plant lists and planting plans for garden and rose garden.
          1 file; 1 roll

JR/1/103 *Cookson, Lt. Col. J.C.V.*
          Meldon Park, Morpeth, Northumberland   1960
          Correspondence, also with estate staff, plant list and planting plan for garden.
          1 file; 1 roll

JR/1/104 *Cooper, Major*
          Russborough House, Dunlewy, co. Donegal, Eire
          nd
          Planting plan for garden.
          1 file

James Russell Archive

JR/1/105 **Corbett, W.**
Dower House, Longnor, Derbyshire 1957
Planting plan of garden.
1 file

JR/1/106 **Cornwall, Duchy of**
Highgrove, Gloucestershire 1985
Correspondence, plant lists and planting plans for gardens.
1 file

JR/1/107 **Cottenham, Earl of**
Hungerhill House, Coolham, Sussex 1956
Correspondence, also with Sunningdale Nurseries, pressed leaf of a virginia creeper, plant list and planting plan for garden.
1 file

JR/1/108 **Cotterell, Sir Richard, Bt.**
Garns, Hereford nd
Planting plan for garden.
1 file

JR/1/109 **Courtauld, S.**
Chieveley Manor, Newbury, Berkshire 1975-1976
Correspondence, plant list and planting plan for garden.
1 file

JR/1/110 **Courtney, Mr Anthony & Mrs Elizabeth, Lady Tregarne**
Pembroke House, Valley End, Chobham, Surrey
1961-1963
Correspondence, plant list and planting plan for garden.
1 file; 1 roll

JR/1/111 **Chrichton, Col. M., and Mrs**
Killyreagh, Tamlaght, near Enniskillen, co. Fermanagh, Northern Ireland 1956-1962
Correspondence, plant list, and planting plans for flower borders and garden.
1 file; 1 roll

James Russell Archive

JR/1/112 *Crichton-Stuart, Major Michael and Mrs,*
Falkland Palace, Fifeshire, Scotland 1959-1962
Correspondence, plant list and planting plan for garden.
1 file

JR/1/113 *Culzean Castle, Maybole, Ayrshire, Scotland*
 1952-1956
Correspondence with W.J. Orr of The Gardens, Culzean Castle, The National Trust for Scotland, and Lady Ferguson of Kilkerran, Maybole, list of expenses, plant lists and planting plans for Fountain Garden and gardens.
1 file; 1 roll

JR/1/114 *d'Abo, R.E.N.*
West Wratting Park, Cambridgeshire 1966
Correspondence, Ordnance Survey map, plant list and planting plan for gardens.
1 file; 1 roll

JR/1/115 *Darwin, Robin*
The Pavillion, Syon Park, Old Isleworth, Middlesex and the Royal College of Art, London 1952-1956
Correspondence, also with the bursar of the Royal College of Art, plant list and planting plans for gardens.
1 file

JR/1/116 *de Hamal, Mrs Constance*
Newton Grange, Newton Regis, near Tamworth, Staffordshire
 1959-1961
Correspondence, plant list and planting plans for garden.
1 file

JR/1/117 *de Quincey, Capt. R.S. and Mrs A.*
The Vern, Marden, Herefordshire 1951-1967
Correspondence, also with Sunningdale, G.E. Gutteridge, Messrs. van Tubergen and others, telegrams, invoices, schedules for work, plant lists and planting plans for garden.
1 file; 1 roll; 1 plan folder

JAMES RUSSELL ARCHIVE

JR/1/118 **Derby, Earl of**
Knowsley Hall, Prescot, Lancashire   1963-1970
Correspondence, also with estate staff and the Hon. Claude Phillimore, Ordnance Survey maps, plant lists and planting plans for rose beds, glade above Dungeon Dam and garden.
1 file; 1 roll

JR/1/119 **de Rothschild, Baronne Edouard and Madame**
Manoir Sans Souci, Rue des Aigles, Chantilly, Oise, France
    1965
Correspondence, plant lists and planting plans.
1 file; 1 roll

JR/1/120 **de Rothschild, Baron Guy**
Chateau de Ferrieres   1956-1957
Correspondence, plant lists, sketches of schemes and planting plans for the garden.
1 file; 1 roll

JR/1/121 **Devonshire, Duke of**
Chatsworth, Bakewell, Derbyshire   1972
Correspondence re. new greenhouse.
1 file

JR/1/122 **Digby, the Hon. Mrs Edward**
Minterne, Dorchester, Dorset   1960
Correspondence, plant list and planting plans for swimming pool and garden.
1 file; 1 roll

JR/1/123 **Drogheda, Earl of**
Parkside House, Englefield Green, Surrey   1959
Correspondence, plant lists and sketch.
1 file

JR/1/124 **Drury-Lowe, Capt. P.**
Locko Park, near Derby, Derbyshire   1966
Correspondence, also with estate staff, plant lists and planting plans for borders.
1 file; 1 roll

James Russell Archive

JR/1/125 *Duff Gordon, Sir Andrew, Bt.*
Harpton Court, Walton, Presteigne, Radnorshire   1966
Correspondence.
1 file

JR/1/126 *Dufferin & Ava, Marchioness Maureen and Judge John Maude*
The Owl House, Lamberhurst, Kent   1954-1967
Correspondence, also with Finmere Construction Co. Ltd., G.S. Thomas, Sir Martyn Beckett and others, quotations, Ordnance Survey map, plant lists and planting plans for heather garden and garden.
1 file; 1 roll; 1 plan folder

JR/1/127 *Dunne, Capt. Thomas and Mrs Henrietta*
Gatley Park, Leinthall Earls, Leominster, Herefordshire
    1963-1984
Correspondence, section of Ordnance Survey map, plant list and planting plans for garden.
1 file; 1 roll; 1 plan folder

JR/1/128 *Dunne, Mrs*
The Old Parsonage, East Clandon, Surrey   nd
Planting plans for borders and garden.
1 file; 1 roll

JR/1/129 *d'Unsel, Comte Philippe*
1a Avenue de la Renaissance, Brussels, Belgium   1967
Correspondence, plant list and planting plan for garden.
1 file; 1 roll

JR/1/130 *de Ramsey, Lord Ailwyn and Lilah*
Abbots Ripton Hall, Huntingdonshire   1972-1978
Correspondence, also with estate staff, S.Y. Geh, Commissioner of Parks and Recreation, Botanic Gardens, Singapore, Dr. V. Seneviratne, Dept. of Botany, Colombo, Sri Lanka, J.P. Foster of Marshall Sisson, the County Planning Officer and the Countryside Commission, various nurseries and others, memoranda, import licences, plant lists, maps and planting plans for tropical and cool plant houses and for trees.
see also JR/1/272, JR/1/393, JR/1/456
4 files

James Russell Archive

JR/1/131 **Elgin, Countess of**
Culross Abbey House, Culross by Dunfermline, Fifeshire, Scotland nd
Planting plans of garden.
1 file; 1 roll

JR/1/132 **Elwes, Col. Guy and Mrs Barbara**
Ham Spray House, Marlborough, Wiltshire 1961-1963
Correspondence, plant list and planting plans for kitchen garden, borders and garden.
1 file; 1 roll

JR/1/133 **Eliot, Lord Peregrine, Earl of St. Germans**
Port Eliot, St. Germans, Cornwall 1978-1992
Correspondence, also with estate staff, and Richard Carew Pole, itinerary, plant lists and plans of house and grounds.
1 file

JR/1/134 **Eton College,**
Eton, Windsor, Berkshire 1956-1960
Correspondence with P. Proby and Mrs. Lambert, draft minutes, Ordnance Survey map, plant lists and planting plans for tree planting, the swimming pool and the Vice-Provost's garden.
1 file; 1 roll

JR/1/135 **Exbury Gardens Ltd**
Exbury Enterprises Ltd, Exbury Estate, Hampshire 1953-1989
Correspondence with Exbury Gardens Ltd, including T. Drew, P.N. Barber, D. Harris, L.A. Stockwell, E. de Rothschild, also in connection with the Seiyo Corporation, Japan, also with G.S. Thomas, Sir E. Saville and F. Wynyate and Sunningdale, price lists, delivery and confirmation notes, invoices, plant lists
1 file

JR/1/136 **Faerber, Mr. S.**
Wedgewood, 110 Rosemary Hill Road, Little Aston, Sutton Coalfield, Warwickshire 1971-1973
Correspondence, also with Messrs. Joseph Bentley Ltd, plant lists and planting plan.
1 file

James Russell Archive

JR/1/137 **Fattorini, D.**
Sawley Hall, near Ripon, Yorkshire　　　1966
Correspondence with plant list and planting plan
1 file; 1 roll

JR/1/138 **Feversham, Anne, Countess of**
Pennyholme, Fadmoor, Yorkshire; Nawton Towers, Helmsley, Yorkshire; Bransdale, Yorkshire; 4 Halkin Street, Belgravia, London　　　1951-1983
Correspondence, also with estate staff, C. Brickell, C.R. St. Q. Wall of the National Trust, G.S. Thomas, S. Adderley, Sir Martyn Beckett, O. Haskard, Sunningdale Nurseries and others, delivery and order notes, plant lists and planting plans for area around gladiator statue, borders and pool garden at Nawton Towers, for bog at Bransdale, for the gardens at Halkin Street, and for borders and grounds at Pennyholme
1 file; 1 roll

JR/1/139 **Findlay, Mrs Eira**
Carnell, Hurlford by Kilmarnock, Ayrshire, Scotland
　　　1974
Correspondence with plant list and planting plans for garden.
1 file

JR/1/140 **FitzAlan, Viscountess, of Derwent**
Houghton Hall, Sancton, Yorkshire　　　1953
Correspondence, plant lists and planting plans for herbaceous border, Italian garden, foot of walled garden and south front of Houghton Hall.
1 file; 1 roll

JR/1/141 **FitzWilliam, Earl**
Milton Hall, Peterborough, Northamptonshire
　　　1952-1954
Correspondence, plant lists and planting plans for rose and peony borders, tree planting and garden.
1 file; 1 roll

JAMES RUSSELL ARCHIVE

JR/1/142 **Fleming, Mr I. and Mrs A.**
Sevenhampton Place, Sevenhampton, Wiltshire and Warneford Place, Sevenhampton, Wiltshire 1961-1979
Correspondence, also with Hobbs & Chambers, Ordnance Survey map, plant lists and planting plans for Warneford Place.
1 file; 1 roll

JR/1/143 **Fletcher-Watson, J.**
The Old Vicarage, Windrush, Gloucestershire 1971
Correspondence, plant list and building and planting plans for garden.
1 file

JR/1/144 **Fortescue, L.S.**
The Garden House, Buckland Monachorum, Yelverton, Devon
1971-1973
Correspondence and order.
1 file; 1 roll

JR/1/145 **Foster, Michael**
Leysthorpe, Osbaldwick, York 1971-1974
Correspondence, plant lists and planting plans for borders and garden.
1 file

JR/1/146 **Foster, Simon M.**
The Egton Estates Company, Estate Office, Egton Bridge, near Whitby, North Yorkshire 1980
Correspondence and map of Egton manor.
1 file

JR/1/147 **Foster, Mrs William**
Lexham Hall, King's Lynn, Norfolk 1958-1963
Correspondence with plant lists and planting plans for garden.
1 file; 1 roll

JR/1/148 **Fuller, Lt. Col. C.**
Jaggards, Corsham, Wiltshire 1975
Correspondence and planting plan for garden.
1 file

JAMES RUSSELL ARCHIVE

JR/1/149 **Funke, Charles**
Charles Funke Associates, Landscape Consultants, 5 Mill Pool House, Mill Lande, Godalming, Surrey; Flower House Display Ltd, 315 Brompton Road, London and Craigwell Nurseries (Guildford) Ltd, 136 Chertsey Lane, Staines, Middlesex
1974-1991
Correspondence, also with F. Flaherty re. Bahrain project and invoices.
1 file

JR/1/150 **Lloyd's Bank Ltd, Bankside Computer Centre** *1976-1978*
Correspondence, also with Craigwell Nurseries, Glyndebourne Festival Opera, Fitzroy, Robinson & Partners, Gleeds Chartered Quantity Surveyors and others, memoranda, invoices, photographs of plants, plant lists and planting plans for terraces, internal and external landscaping.
1 file

JR/1/151 **Galle, Fred C., Horticultural Consultant**
Hamilton, Georgia and Callaway Gardens, Ida Cason Calloway Foundation, Pine Mountain, Georgia, USA *1980-1987*
Correspondence, including invitation for visit to China, plant labels, and plant lists.
1 file

JR/1/152 **Galliers-Pratt, Mr A.M. and Mrs**
Mawley Hall, Cleobury Mortimer, via Kidderminster, Worcestershire and Whitwell Hall, Whitwell-on-the-hill, Yorkshire *1952-1965*
Correspondence, delivery notes, plant lists, Ordnance Survey map and planting plans for avenue, forecourt, beds, borders and garden at Mawley Hall and shrub and borders, the glade garden at Whitwell Hall.
1 file; 1 roll

JR/1/153 **Galliers-Pratt, G.K.**
Sutton Hall, Sutton on the Forest, Yorkshire *1953-1954*
Correspondence, Ordnance Survey plan, plant list and planting plans for shrub border, terrace and woodland ride.
1 file

James Russell Archive

JR/1/154 **Gardiner, N.W.**
Great Auclum, Burghfield Common, Berkshire 1959-1960
Correspondence, plant list and planting plan for garden of Mawley Hall. Catalogue '1959-60 Price List of Rhododendrons & Azaleas' Sunningdale Nurseries.
1 file

JR/1/155 **Geddes, F.**
Havenfield, Great Missenden, Buckinghamshire 1958-1961
Correspondence, plant list and planting plans for grove copse and gardens.
1 file; 1 roll

JR/1/156 **Gee, Hilary**
University of Keele, Keele, Staffordshire 1973
Correspondence.
1 file

JR/1/157 **German, Mrs Guy**
Brocton Lodge, near Stafford, Staffordshire 1965-1966
Correspondence, plant lists and planting plans for garden.
1 file; 1 roll

JR/1/158 **Gibson, Mrs J.W.**
Maryville, Croom, Co. Limerick, Eire 1954-1956
Correspondence, orders, invoices, plant lists and planting plans for tree planting, box garden and garden.
1 file; 1 roll

JR/1/159 **Gibson-Fleming, Major and Mrs Selina**
Ranston, Blandford, Dorset 1964-1976
Correspondence and planting plan for garden.
1 file; 1 roll

JR/1/160 **Garnett, Mrs A.M. and Kit, formerly Mrs A.M. Govett & John**
Fosbury Manor, Marlborough, Wiltshire and Glenbogle Lodge, Banchory, Kincardineshire 1956-1962
Correspondence, plant list, Ordnance Survey map and planting schemes for gardens at Fosbury Manor and Glenbogle Lodge.
1 box, 2 rolls

JAMES RUSSELL ARCHIVE

JR/1/161 **Gilmour, Lady Caroline**
The Ferry House, Isleworth, Middlesex and Lion Place, [2 Wilton Row, London] 1965
Correspondence, also with Sunningdale Nurseries, quotation, plant lists and planting plans for both gardens.
1 file, 1 roll

JR/1/162 **Gisborough, Lord and Lady**
Gisborough House, Guisborough, Cleveland 1973-1981
Correspondence, also with R.V. Roger Ltd., plant list and planting plans for tennis court, Guisborough Hall and garden.
1 file

JR/1/163 **Godsal, Alan and Elizabeth**
Haines Hill, Twyford, Berkshire 1962-1986
Correspondence, Ordnance Survey map, invoices, plant list, sketches, map, and building and planting plans for swimming pool and garden.
1 file; 1 roll

JR/1/164 **Gordon-Lennox, Mrs**
Gordon Castle, Fochabers, Morayshire 1963-1964
Correspondence, plant lists and planting plan for Gordon Castle.
1 file; 1 roll

JR/1/165 **Granville, Earl**
Callernish House, Sollas, North Uist, Outer Hebrides, Inverness-shire, Scotland 1964-1967
Correspondence, also with V. Russell Smith, Monro Horticultural Sundries Ltd., the Unique Dutch Light Co. Ltd., and various nurseries, booklet 'Field Trial Results' by the North of Scotland College of Agriculture, plant lists and planting plans for kitchen garden, beds and garden.
1 file; 1 roll

JR/1/166 **Green, Mrs Robert**
6017 La Salle Avenue, Oakland, California, USA 1973-1975
Correspondence.
1 file

James Russell Archive

JR/1/167 *Griffiths, Mrs D.H.*
Garthmeilio, Llangwym, Corwen, Merionethshire, Wales
1973
Correspondence, plant list and planting plans for garden.
1 file

JR/1/168 *Grose, Mrs*
49 Elyston Court, London 1975
Correspondence and plant list.
1 file

JR/1/169 *Grosvenor, Col. R.G. and Mrs Viola*
Ely Lodge, Enniskillen, Co. Fermanagh, Northern Ireland
1956-1962
Correspondence, plant lists and planting plans for glade, borders, terrace and garden.
1 file; 1 roll

JR/1/170 *Gunston, Lady*
The Watch House, Bembridge, Isle of Wight 1958-1962
Correspondence, plant lists and planting plan for the garden.
1 file; 1 roll

JR/1/171 *General Accident, Fire and Life Assurance Corporation Ltd*
Head Office, Pitheavlis, Perthshire 1963-1984
Correspondence, also with James Parr and Partners, architects, James Laurie & Sons, John Horsman, Toro Irrigation with promotional folder, Urban Planters with promotional material, A.C. Rentaplant with promotional material, Exbury Gardens Ltd, Hydon Nurseries Ltd, with orders, meteorological reports at Wellshill Cemetery, Perth, minutes, plant lists and building and planting plans for roof gardens, terraces, courtyards, internal and external landscaping.
1 box; 10 rolls

JR/1/172 *Haddon-Paton, Major A.G.N.*
Rossway, Berkhamstead, Hertfordshire 1981
Correspondence and plant list re the Ashbridge Arboretum, National Trust.
1 file

James Russell Archive

JR/1/173 **Haddington, Countess of, Sarah**
Tyninghame, Dunbar, East Lothian, Scotland   1955-1966
Correspondence, also with estate staff and Sunningdale Nurseries, Ordnance Survey maps, plant lists, sketches and planting plans for the sand dunes, the walled garden, rose walk and garden.
1 file; 1 roll

JR/1/174 **Hague, Major Derek**
Denchworth Manor, Berkshire   1956
Ordnance Survey map and planting plans for garden.
1 file; 1 roll

JR/1/175 **Haig, Countess**
Bemersyde, St. Boswells, Melrose, Roxburghshire, Scotland
1964
Correspondence, plant list and planting plan for garden.
1 file; 1 roll

JR/1/176 **Halifax, Earl**
Garrowby Hall, Garrowby, Humberside   1980-1983
Correspondence, also with estate staff, Firma C. Esveld, R.V. Roger Ltd., F.F. Johnson & Partners and others, invoices, soil analysis, plant list, part of Ordnance Survey map and planting plans for water garden, gardens, park land and estate.
1 file; 1 roll

JR/1/177 **Halifax, Dowager Countess of**   1971
Correspondence with Anne, Countess of Feversham, Pennyholme, Fadmore, with plant list and plans for her mother's garden at Bugthorpe.
1 file

JR/1/178 **Hall, P.**
Longford Hall, Newport, Shropshire   1964
Correspondence, Ordnance Survey map, plant list and planting plans for beds and lakes.
1 file; 1 roll

JAMES RUSSELL ARCHIVE

JR/1/179 **Hambleden, Lady**
The Manor House, Hambleden, Henley on Thames, Oxfordshire
1964
Correspondence, plant list and planting plans for rose garden.
1 file; 1 roll

JR/1/180 **Hambleden, Viscount**
The Manor House, Hambleden, Henley on Thames, Oxfordshire
1980
Correspondence.
1 file

JR/1/181 **Hampshire Gardens Trust**
Jermyns House Appeal, Hillier Arboretum, Ampfield, Hampshire
1987
Correspondence with P.S. Middleton of Hampshire County Council, Mrs. Maldwin Drummond, John McCarthy and Gill Headley, and promotional pack: 'The Hillier Arboretum Charitable Trust'.
See also JR/1/199
1 file

JR/1/182 **Hanbury-Williams, Mr J.M.A. and Mrs D.**
Huxley Lane Farm, Huxley, near Chester, Cheshire
1970-1972
Correspondence, plant lists and planting plans for garden.
1 file

JR/1/183 **Hare, the Hon. John**
Cottage Farm, Little Blakenham, Ipswich, Suffolk
1958-1959
Correspondence, plant lists and planting plans for garden.
1 file

JR/1/184 **Hill, Derek**
St. Columb, Churchill, co. Donegal, Eire   **1954-1972**
Correspondence, also with Sunningdale Nurseries, plant lists and planting plans for garden.
1 file; 1 roll

JAMES RUSSELL ARCHIVE

JR/1/185 **Hill, A. Robin I.**
Clifton Castle, Ripon, Yorkshire　　　　1970-1971
Correspondence, plant list and planting plans for swimming pool and garden. Correspondence and minutes for Mental Health Trust, Flower Festival Committee.
1 file

JR/1/186 **Holland-Hibbert, the Hon. J. and Mrs I.**
Munden, Watford, Hertfordshire　　　　1968
Correspondence and plant lists.
1 file

JR/1/187 **Hindlip, Viscountess**
Botches, Wivelsfield Green, Sussex　　　　nd
Ordnance Survey plan and planting plan of borders.
1 file; 1 roll

JR/1/188 **Holderness, Lord Richard**
Flat Top House, Bishop Wilton, Humberside　　　1981
Correspondence and planting plan for garden.
1 file

JR/1/189 **Holt Memorial Garden, Liverpool, Lancashire**
　　　　1961-1970
Correspondence with Ocean Management Services Ltd, G.P. Holt of The Ocean Steam Ship Co. Ltd, Messrs. Alfred Holt & Co. Ltd, V. Russell Smith, Stott & Ward Ltd, Dr F.G. Meyer, Sunningdale Nurseries, Charles L. Warren Ltd, staff of the department for Parks and Open Spaces for the county borough of Birkenhead and others, estimates, plant lists, sketches and planting plans.
3 files; 1 roll

JR/1/190 **Hope, Lady John**
Grey's Cottage, Rotherfield Grey's, Oxfordshire
　　　　nd
Planting plans for garden.
1 file

JAMES RUSSELL ARCHIVE

JR/1/191 ***Horder Arthritic Centre, Crowborough, Sussex
and the Marchioness of Dufferin and Ava, Windmill Farm,
Crowborough, Sussex*** 1962-1964
Correspondence, also with Finmere Construction Co. Ltd, Sunningdale Nurseries, Tilhill Forestry (Crowborough) Ltd, H. Pannett (Eastbourne) Ltd, James A. Crabtree & Associates and Dickhampton (Earth Moving) Ltd, soil analysis, plant list and planting plans for both gardens.
1 file; 1 plan folder

JR/1/192 ***Horlick, Col. Sir James
Achamore House, Isle of Gigha, Argyllshire, Scotland and Timbers, Nuffield, near Henley on Thames, Oxfordshire***
1955-1980
Correspondence, also with Messenger & Co. Ltd, Sunningdale Nurseries and others, plant lists and planting plans for herbaceous border and garden at Timbers and for the gardens at Achamore House.
1 file; 1 roll

JR/1/193 ***Horton, Mrs
Three Gates House, Moreton Morrell, Warwickshire***
1966
Correspondence and planting plan for tree clearings etc.
1 file; 1 roll

JR/1/194 ***Hosta & Hemerocallis Society (British)*** 1981-1983
Correspondence with D. Grenfell and R.M. Kitchingham, plant lists, draft of constitution and rules of society and newsletters nos. 1-3.
1 file

JR/1/195 ***Hotchkin, N.S.
Wormersley House, Woodhall Spa, Lindsey, Lincolnshire***
1957-1965
Correspondence, also with Sunningdale Nurseries, plant lists, building and planting plans for borders and the garden.
1 file; 1 roll

James Russell Archive

JR/1/196 **Howard de Walden, Lady**
Wonham Manor, Bletchworth, Surrey 1959-1962
Correspondence, with holiday itinerary, Ordnance Survey maps, plant list and planting plans for The Glade, pool garden, herbaceous border and the garden.
1 file; 1 roll

JR/1/197 **Howell, J. Bede, West Midland Woodlands**
15 Broad Street, Pershore, Worcestershire 1985
Correspondence and list of nurseries' addresses.
1 file

JR/1/198 **Hurst, Mrs Margery**
Flutters Hill, Longcross, near Chertsey, Surrey nd
Planting plan for garden.
1 file; 1 roll

JR/1/199 **Hillier Arboretum, Ampfield, Hampshire** 1972-1988
Correspondence with members involved with the Hillier Arboretum including the Hillier family and Hillier Nurseries (Winchester) Ltd, the Earl of Carnarvon, C.D. Brickell, M. Mason, Hampshire County Council, agendas and minutes of Hillier Arboretum Management Committee, Standing Advisory Panel, Jermyns House Appeal Think Tank, Landscape Sub-Committee, copies of trust deeds, plant lists, promotional literature, personnel file; including applications, for appointment of curator in 1984, Ordnance Survey map, building and planting plans.
See also JR/1/181
2 boxes; 1 roll

JR/1/200 **Harmsworth, the Hon. Vere**
Stroods, Heron's Ghyll, near Uckfield, Sussex 1963
Correspondence re. swimming pool.
1 file; 1 roll

JR/1/201 **Harris, J. Gordon S.**
Mallet Court Nursery, Curry Mallett, Taunton, Somerset
1969-1989
Correspondence and Mallet Court Nursery plant lists.
1 file; 1 roll

JR/1/202 Smithers, Sir P.; Henderson, N., Haskard; Oliver of Bowyers Nurseries, Liss, Hampshire   1969-1973

Correspondence and invoices relating to the following people: P. Smithers, E.P. Webb, E.E. Barbour, J. Profumo, J. Burgett, Lady Mowbray & Stourton, Messrs Keir & Cawdor Ltd, H.P. McIlhenny, P. Cox, Countess Jellicoe, Mrs Sanders, Mrs Raversley, Mrs B.A.C. Whitmee, Sir Sacheverell Sitwell, Mrs Butler, S.F.T.L. Robinson, C. Brocklehurst, Marchioness of Cholmondeley, Mrs. Cathie, E. Mackenzie, F.G. Barker, N. Henderson, Major S. Baillie, Mrs V. Willis, J. Keswick, Major D. Butter, M. Brockway, N. Broackes, Major P. Miller-Mundy, O. Haskard, and R.F. Sanderson.
1 file; 1 roll

JR/1/203 Hastings, Lord
Seaton Delaval Hall, Northumberland   1950-1953

Correspondence, also with estate staff, Claude Phillimore, Messrs. Rawlence & Squarey, D. Higgins and Sunningdale Nurseries, plant lists, sketches, section of Ordnance Survey map and planting plans for the parterre and garden.
1 file; 1 roll

JR/1/204 Heathcoat-Amory, Brigadier R.
Osbaldwick Hall, Yorkshire   1972-1975

Correspondence, plant list and planting plans for garden.
1 box; 1 roll

JR/1/205 Henderson, J.P.R.
West Woodhay House, Newbury, Berkshire   1952-1982

Correspondence, also with Sutton Griffin & Partners, pressed petal of rhododendron, invoices, plant lists and planting plans for memorial garden of Sarah Henderson, borders and garden.
1 file; 1 roll

JR/1/206 Holliday, Mrs L.B.
Mount St John, Thirsk, Yorkshire   1971

Correspondence and planting plan for garden.
1 file; 1 roll

JAMES RUSSELL ARCHIVE

JR/1/207 **Herdman, Mrs Dorothy**
Carricklee House, Strabane, co. Tyrone, Eire 1953-1958
Correspondence, also with Sunningdale Nurseries, J.G. Burns, Slieve Donard Nurseries Co. Ltd, statement of account, plant lists and planting plans for shrub border and garden.
1 file; 1 roll

JR/1/208 **Hildyard, Myles, T.**
Flintham Hall, Newark, Nottinghamshire 1955-1970
Correspondence.
1 file

JR/1/209 **Horsman, John, Fyne Trees & Plus Trees**
Cairndow, Argyll, Scotland, formerly Torrisdale, Campbeltown, Argyllshire, Scotland 1979-1991
Correspondence, plant lists, catalogues and promotional literature, including 'The Pinetum'.
1 file

JR/1/210 **Heseltine, Rt. Hon. Michael R.D.**
Thenford House, near Banbury, Oxfordshire 1989-1990
Correspondence and notes.
1 file

JR/1/211 **Internationales Burgen-Institut Historical Gardens Exhibition**
1979
Correspondence with members of Internationales Burgen-Institut and staff at Castle Howard re. 1980 Gardens Exhibition.
1 file

JR/1/212 **Ilchester, Countess of**
Melbury House, Dorchester, Dorset 1956-1957
Plant lists, Ordnance Survey map and building and planting plans for orangery, formal garden, lake, parkside and garden.
1 file; 1 roll

JR/1/213 **Information, useful** 1948
Correspondence with M. Montrose, F. Watson of The Wallace Collection, London, Exbury Estates, relatives, V. Russell Smith, 'Amateur Gardening' and W.L. & H. Collingridge Ltd, H.J. Hatfield & Sons Ltd, M.R. Birdsey, Fife County Council, Glasshouse Crops Research Institiute; quotations, invoices and receipts; plant lists; reports: 'Sunningdale Nurseries 1939-49'; instructions manuals.
1 file

JR/1/214 **Insurance** 1972-1985
Correspondence with Hogg Robinson (U.K.) Ltd, Sun Alliance & London Insurance Group, Lombard North Central Ltd, insurance confirmations and other documents, copy of Business Development Loan Agreement, copy of registration for VAT, Health and Safety at Work notice for Castle Howard.
1 file

JR/1/215 **James, the Hon. David and Jacquetta**
Torosay Castle, Isle of Mull, Scotland, and Townings Place, Wivelsfield Green, near Haywards Heath, Sussex
1957-1980
Correspondence, also with estate staff, plant lists, section of Ordnance Survey map and planting plans for gardens.
1 file; 1 roll

JR/1/216 **Jarvie, R.W.G.**
Fairfield Lodge, Bothwell, Glasgow, Scotland
1971
Correspondence, plant list and planting plans for garden.
1 file

JR/1/217 **Jellicoe, Earl George and Countess Phillipa**
Tidcombe Manor, near Marlborough, Wiltshire
1961-1990
Correspondence, plant lists and planting plans for 'tropical cornucopia', vegetable garden, rose garden, beech walk, pleached walk and garden.
1 file

JAMES RUSSELL ARCHIVE

JR/1/218 **Jenks, D. Brian**
Astbury Hall, Bridgenorth, Shropshire   1961-1962
Correspondence, Ordnance Survey map, plant lists and planting plans for garden.
1 file; 1 roll

JR/1/219 **Jenyns, Mrs Kathleen**
The Grange, Huttons Ambo, North Yorkshire   1984-1985
Correspondence, also with Exbury Gardens Ltd, plant list and planting plans for garden.
1 file

JR/1/220 **Hare, the Hon. John**
Cottage Farm, Little Blakenham, Ipswich, Suffolk
                                                                                1958-1959
Correspondence, plant lists and planting plans for garden.
1 file

JR/1/222 **Daily Mail Ideal Homes Exhibition, 1963**   1962-1963
Correspondence with A. Whitehead, Mr. Thomas, W.G. Jones, L.R. Trevor Smith, T. Hopewell-Ash and other individuals involved with the exhibition, Messrs F. de Jong, Exbury Gardens, Messrs Stuart Low & Co. Ltd, Impetus Garden Furniture Ltd, Dowdeswells (1930) Ltd, Biddles Ltd, 'House & Garden', Thomas Rochford & Sons Ltd, Constance Spry Ltd, Sunningdale Nurseries, Mr A. Caiger-Smith of The Potteries at Aldermaston, Robert Green Gerard Ltd, John Sander, Geo. Monro (Flowers) Ltd, Verine Products & Co., John Keswick, Sir Eric Savill, Caledonian Nurseries, Messrs Walter Blom & Sons Ltd, Messrs Evans, Messrs I.W. Cole & Son, Messrs Forbes, Gordon Baldwin, Kendell Stone & Paving Co. Ltd, Messrs R. Panichelli & Sons, Girling Stone Ltd. Also photographs of garden furniture, pots and saucers, features, sketches of structures with exhibition, design and planting plans, map of exhibition, promotional literature 'The Orangery designed & planted by James Russell, the Sunningdale Nurseries', quotations, orders, despatch notes, expenses and receipts.
1 file

JAMES RUSSELL ARCHIVE

JR/1/223 **Daily Mail Ideal Homes Exhibition, 1974**   1973-1974
Correspondence with L.R. Trevor Smith, T. Hopewell-Ash and exhibition staff, Brigadier N.S. Cowan of the Waddesdon Estate, Lady Labouchere, Lord de Ramsey, Burnside Nursery, Exbury Gardens Ltd, Sunningdale Nurseries, MAT Transport Ltd, Paul Temple Ltd, Van Tubergen Ltd, John Keswick, work programme, orders, invoices, plant lists, sketch of exhibition, exhibition and planting plans.
1 file

JR/1/224 **Mount Agaki Nature Observation Park, Japan**   1987-1991
Correspondence with Mr Minoru Aria, Mr Hiroyuki Arimasa, Mr. Satoshi Arisaka, Yuji Kurashige, Hiroyuki Sato, Hisayori Abe, M. Yagi, Hideaki Fuse, Hideo Suzuki, Peter K. Okada, Mr Hiroshi Tsushi, Mr Takashi Suzuki, Tsuneo Nakamura, Tsunekata Naito, Miss Fumiko Tsuzuki, Mrs Keiko Fujimoto of the Seiyo Corporation, the Seibu Akagi Botanical Institute, Principal Alp Designesr Inc., and Nozawa/Suzuki Partnership, as well as Glendoick Gardens, E.G. Millais, Tsunekat Naito, John D. Bond, Notcutts Nurseries Ltd, Hillier Nurseries, Peter Foggo of Arup Associates, RHS Enterprises, Miki Travel Agency, Edmund de Rothschild, Miriam Rothschild, C.D. Brickell, G. Taaffe, Red Lion Bookshop, Exbury Enterprises Ltd, Kazuko Yahiro editor of the RHS of Japan, RHS Japan newsletters no. 3 1989/4, no. 6 1989/10 and no. 10 1990/7, itineraries, plant lists, maps of Mount Agaki and planting plans, photographs of plantings.
2 boxes, 3 rolls

JR/1/225 **Chris Chadwell, Kashmir**   1983-1986
Correspondence, also with A.P.C. Powell, application forms, plant lists and promotional literature for plant hunting expeditions, talks and lecture tours.
1 file

JR/1/226 **Keith, Kenneth, Lord of Castleacre**
The Wicken House, Castleacre, near King's Lynn, Norfolk
   1957-1982
Correspondence, also with staff, Fisher & Sons (Fakenham) Ltd, and Francis Egerton, photographs of statues, sketch for pool house, plant lists, and planting plans for flower borders, swimming pool and the garden.
1 file; 1 roll

JAMES RUSSELL ARCHIVE

JR/1/227 **Keith, David A. & Caroline**
West Barsham Hall, Fakenham, Norfolk   1958-1973
Correspondence, delivery notes, plant lists and planting plans for herbaceous border and the garden, including lower and upper pair of borders.
1 file; 1 roll

JR/1/228 **Kent, H.R.H. the Duchess of**
Anmer Hall, Anmer, near King's Lynn, Norfolk   1973-1975
Correspondence, also with staff, Sunningdale Nurseries, Woods Landscapes and Van Tubergen, invoices, plant lists, section of Ordnance Survey map, and planting plans.
1 file

JR/1/229 **Ker, David**
Fisherton Delamere House, Warminster, Wiltshire   1981
Correspondence, plant lists and planting plans for border, driveway and garden. House was formerly owned by Mrs. Blake-Tyler, for whom James Russell designed the garden.
See also JR/1/44
1 file; 1 roll

JR/1/230 **Kern, Joseph, J. Rose Nusery**
Box 33, Mentor, Ohio, USA   1973-1974
Correspondence, plant lists and catalogues for roses at the Joseph J. Kern Rose Nursery: 'Old Roses New Fall 1972 - Spring 1973', 'Old Roses New Fall 1974 - Spring 1975'.
1 file

JR/1/231 **Keswick, John and Clare**
Portrack House, Holywood, Dumfriesshire, Scotland
1961-1985
Correspondence, also with staff, David Keswick, Beth Chatto, W.R. Hean, principal of Threave School of Practical Gardening, Messrs Christies (Fochabers) Ltd, Hilliers & Sons (Winchester) Ltd, Messrs John Waterer, Sons & Crisp Ltd, notes on 'China Roses brought to Kew and Portrack November 1979/80', travel itinerary, invoices, photographs of roses, plant lists and planting plans for shelter belt, Glengower Wood, Crow Wood, and garden.
see also JR/1/232
1 file; 1 roll

James Russell Archive

JR/1/232 **Keswick, Maggie**
11 Park Walk, Chelsea, London 1973
Correspondence re. conversion of balcony into greenhouse.
see also, JR/1/231
1 file

JR/1/233 **Khaled, King**
Ryhad 1978
Correspondence with Major P.N. Barber and planting plan of greenhouse for King Khaled.
1 file

JR/1/234 **Kinmouth, Fergus**
32 Royal Crescent Mews, London 1990
Correspondence, promotional literature re trip to Bhutan and photocopies of articles relating to oaks.
1 file

JR/1/235 **Kirkwood, Sir Robert**
Haven House, Sandwich, Kent 1965-1967
Correspondence, also with staff, V. Russell Smith and Sunningdale Nurseries, plant lists and planting plans for picking beds and the garden.
1 file; 1 roll

JR/1/236 **Kinnersley, Charles**
Carrick Cottage, Stronguet Point, Feock, near Truro, Cornwall
1963-1966
Correspondence, plant lists and planting plans for borders, beds and the garden.
1 file; 1 roll

JR/1/237 **Kimball, Marcus M.P.**
Great Easton Manor, Market Harborough, Leicestershire
1961-1964
Correspondence, plant list and planting plans for shrub border, and the garden.
1 file; 1 roll

Page from a Sunningdale Nursery Catalogue c. early 1960s.

Source: Russell archive, Borthwick Institute, University of York [JR/1/77]

The Parterre at Seaton Delaval Hall. Designed by James Russell (his first major project) for Lord Hastings in 1950.

Source: Lord Hastings

Archway with metal gate and roses either side – Castle Howard. Garden designer: James Russell.

Source: Fritz von der Schulenburg – The Interior Archive

View to the urn at Rudding Park. Garden designed by James Russell and Sir Everard Radcliffe in the 1960s.

Source: Rudding Park

James Russell in the Rose Garden at Castle Howard with pyramid shaped rose trellis with pink roses.

Source: Fritz von der Schulenburg – The Interior Archive

James Russell sitting against the edge of his table in the Garden Room, The Dairies, on the Castle Howard Estate.
Source: Fritz von der Schulenburg - The Interior Archive

Basingstoke – Wiggins Teape building by Arrups 1977. Planting design James Russell.
Source: Lucinda Lambton / Arcaid

James Russell Archive

JR/1/238 **Kennedy, Mrs**
Nether Underwood, by Kilmarnock, Ayrshire, Scotland
    1958-1960
Correspondence, plant list and planting plan for the garden.
1 file

JR/1/239 **Labouchere, Lady Rachel**
Dudmaston, Bridgnorth, Shropshire   1973-1975
Correspondence, plant lists and planting plans for the garden
1 file

JR/1/240 **Lambton, Lady Elizabeth**
Mortimer Hill, Mortimer, Berkshire   1956-1957
Correspondence, sketch of urn, plant lists and planting plans for the garden.
1 file; 1 roll

JR/1/241 **Lancaster, Osbert & Anne**
Aldworth, near Streatley-on-Thames, Berkshire; 12 Eaton Square, London and 78 Cheyne Court, Royal Hospital Road, London
    1968-1986
Correspondence, plant lists and planting plans for garden at Aldworth.
1 file

JR/1/242 **Lansdale, David**
Dalswinton, Dumfriesshire, Scotland and Gigha, Argyllshire, Scotland   1979
Correspondence re. Gigha.
1 file

JR/1/243 **Lansdale, Mrs Beatrice**
Dalswinton, Dumfriesshire, Scotland   1961-1968
Correspondence, plant lists and planting plans for picking border and garden.
1 file; 1 roll

JAMES RUSSELL ARCHIVE

JR/1/244 **Lane Fox, Mrs**
The Little House, Bramham Park, Wetherby, West Yorkshire
1973-1975
Correspondence, also with Smiths Gore, Mr Dickinson and Charles Funke, plant lists, Ordnance Survey map and planting plans for Queens Hollow and garden.
1 file

JR/1/245 **Lambert, Uvedale**
South Park, Blechingley, Surrey   1969-1974
Correspondence, plant lists and planting plans.
1 file

JR/1/246 **Lascelles, Hon. Mrs G.**
Fort Belvedere   1956
Planting plans for garden.
1 file; 1 roll

JR/1/247 **Lazenby, Mrs Rosemary**
Fosse Wold, Stow-on-the-Wold, Gloucestershire   1967
Correspondence.
1 file; 1 roll

JR/1/248 **Lecoufle, Marcel**
Marcel Lecoufle Orchidees, 5 Rue de Paris, Booissy Saint Leger, Paris, France   1972-1981
Correspondence, also with Paul Denesvre, invoices and plant lists.
1 file

JR/1/249 **Leitrim, Countess of, Anne**
Mulroy, Carrigart, co. Donegal, Eire   1953-1979
Correspondence, also with estate staff, Sunningdale Nurseries, County Donegal Railways, and the British Transport Commission, invoices, orders and plant lists.
1 file

JR/1/250 **Leveson-Gower, Mrs R.**
Sleningford Grange, Ripon, North Yorkshire   1975
Correspondence, plant lists and planting plans for garden.
1 file

James Russell Archive

JR/1/251 **Leveson, Mrs A.**
Broadlands 1955
Planting plan for garden.
1 file; 1 roll

JR/1/252 **Limberlost Nurseries, J.F. Jones**
PO Freshwater, Cairns, North Queensland, Australia
1972-1973
Correspondence, orders, invoices, also from Van Tubergen, receipts for mail transfer, statements of account, plant lists, price indexes, information sheet and catalogue: 'Limberlost Orchid Seedlings March 1973'.
1 file

JR/1/253 **Lindsay, Hon. Lady Loelia of Dowhill, Duchess of Westminster**
The Old Vicarage, Send, near Woking, Surrey 1959-1972
Correspondence, also mentioning the Yvonne Arnaud Theatre, and with estate staff, plant lists and planting plan for around garage.
1 file; 1 roll

JR/1/254 **Lovell, Sir Bernard**
University of Manchester, Nuffield Radio Astronomy Laboratories, Jodrell Bank, Macclesfield, Cheshire and The Quinta, Swettenham, Cheshire 1979-1989
Correspondence, about lectures, plants, visits and the Jodrell Bank Arboretum, and plant list.
1 file

JR/1/255 **Lowry-Corry, Major Monty**
The Grange, Bembridge, Isle of Wight 1960-1965
Correspondence, plant lists and planting plans for garden.
1 file; 1 roll

JR/1/256 **Loyd, C.L.**
Lockinge, Wantage, Berkshire 1959-1960
Correspondence, also with Sunningdale Nurseries, plant lists and planting plan for border.
1 file; 1 roll

James Russell Archive

JR/1/257 **Lucas, Otto**
Hush Heath Manor, Goudhurst, Kent 1957-1962
Correspondence, also with staff and Sunningdale Nurseries, plant lists and planting plans for garden.
1 file

JR/1/258 **Lumsden, G.R.C.**
Balfour, Menmuir, Brechin, Angus, Scotland 1956-1958
Correspondence, plant lists and planting plans for shrub border and garden.
1 file; 1 roll

JR/1/259 **MacKenzie, Eric & Elizabeth**
Calgary House, Tobermory, Isle of Mull, Argyllshire, Scotland
1958-1966
Correspondence, also with Sunningdale Nurseries, plant lists and planting plans for borders and garden.
1 file

JR/1/260 **MacDonald, Hon. Mrs M.**
Ballaig by Crieff, Perthshire, Scotland 1970
Correspondence, plant list and planting plan for garden.
1 file

JR/1/261 **Mackie, Hon. Mrs Alan**
Enterkine House, Annbank, Ayrshire, Scotland 1964
Correspondence, plant list and planting plans for garden.
1 file; 1 roll

JR/1/262 **MacPherson-Grant, Sir Euan Bt.**
Craigo by Montrose, Angus, Scotland nd
Ordnance Survey map, planting plans for new vista.
1 file; 1 roll

JAMES RUSSELL ARCHIVE

JR/1/263 **Magnolia Society (America)**   1984-1985
Correspondence with Charles E. Tubesing and Harold C. Hopkin, and copies of the following articles:
'Magnolia Zenii: A Rare Magnolia Recently Introduced Into Cultivation' - T.R. Dudley, from vol. 19, no. 1, 1983 of the 'Magnolia Journal of the American Magnolia Society'
'Magnolia Zenii' - P. Del Tredici, from vol. 19, no. 1, 1983 of the 'Magnolia Journal of the American Magnolia Society'
'Sargentiana Robusta: Mulitpetal' - P. Smithers, from vol. 19, no. 1, 1983 of the 'Magnolia Journal of the American Magnolia Society
'!Viva Dealbata!' and letter by J. Rzedowski to H. Hopkins, from vol. 11, no. 2, 1975 of the 'Newsletter of the American Magnolia Society'
Letter to G.A. Pfaffman from J.C. McDaniel, from vol. 11, no. 2, 1975 of the 'Newsletter of the American Magnolia Society'
'A Trip to see the rare Mexican magnolia tree species Magnolia Dealbata' by G.A. Pfaffman, from vol. 11, no. 2, 1975 of the 'Newsletter of the American Magnolia Society'
Letter to Prof. J.C. McDaniel from Harold Hopkins, from vol. 11, no. 2, 1975 of the 'Newsletter of the American Magnolia Society'
'A Progress Report from McDaniel', from vol. 11, no. 2, 1975 of the 'Newsletter of the American Magnolia Society'
'Paying a call on Dealbata' by Tom Dodd III, from vol. 16, no. 1, 1980, of 'Magnolia'
1 file

JR/1/264 **Major, John**
Castle Howard, North Yorkshire   1986-1990
Correspondence, also with Eileen Powton, Alan Mitchell, D.J. Sales, C.D. Brickell, Simon Howard, about the grounds at Castle Howard, including Ray Wood and the Arboretum, the Dairies and James Russell's engagements, promotional literature, plant lists and planting plans for Ray Wood, the Arboretum and Castle Howard grounds.
see also JR/1/459
1 file

JR/1/265 **Malone, Bob**
R.S.D. 106A, Lapoinya, Tasmania   1982-1984
Correspondence, also with Rob Radford, and phytosanitary certificate.
1 file

JAMES RUSSELL ARCHIVE

JR/1/266 **Mander, Sir Charles Bt.**
Little Barrow, Moreton-in-the-Marsh, Gloucestershire
1962
Planting plans for garden.
1 file; 1 roll

JR/1/267 **Mann, George and Margaret**
The Old Rectory, West Woodhay, near Newbury, Berkshire
1961-1965
Correspondence, plant lists and planting plans for garden.
1 file; 1 roll

JR/1/268 **Mann, Lady Clare**
Thelveton Hall, Diss, Norfolk   1973-1974
Correspondence, plant list and planting plan for garden.
1 file

JR/1/269 **Mansfield, Earl of**
Scone Palace, Perth, Scotland   1981-1983
Correspondence, also with estate staff, plant lists and planting plans for area around laburnum tunnel and garden. Also 'Report on the Pinetum & its extension at Scone Palace' by John Horsman with planting plan.
1 file; 1 roll

JR/1/270 **Manton, Mary, Lady**
Houghton Hall, Sancton, Yorkshire   nd
Planting plan.
1 file

JR/1/271 **Marks, Mrs Ann**
Hammill Farm, Eastry, Sandwich, Kent and Asdale, Hascombe, Surrey   1956-1968
Correspondence, also with staff and others, plant lists and planting plans for gardens.
1 file, 1 roll

JAMES RUSSELL ARCHIVE

JR/1/272 **Marks, J.F.E., resident agent for Abbots Ripton**
The Estate Office, Ramsey, Huntingdon   1975-1976
Correspondence, also with Messrs Marshall Sisson (architects), E.S.G. Sales Ltd, M.J. Allen & Sons Ltd.
see also JR/1/130, JR/1/393
1 file

JR/1/273 **Markwell, P., propagator**
Quaymount Ltd, The Nurseries, Row Cottage, Wereham, King's Lynn, Norfolk   1981-1987
Correspondence, also with C.R. Markwell, about propogation etc., plant lists, availability list August 1987.
1 file

JR/1/274 **Marecco, Anthony and Anne**
Port Hall, co. Donegal, Eire   1956-1964
Correspondence, plant list and planting plans for borders and garden.
1 file; 1 roll

JR/1/275 **Marston, David and Joan K., fern specialist**
Culag, Green Lane, Nafferton, Driffield, Humberside
    1974-1984
Correspondence, plant lists and catalogue of ferns.
1 file

JR/1/276 **Mauritius - Government Centre**   1979
Correspondence with Fry, Drew, Knight & Creamer, building and planting plans.
1 file

JR/1/277 **May, Hugh and Betty**
Ryders Wells Farm, near Lewes, Sussex   1972
Correspondence and plant list.
1 file

JAMES RUSSELL ARCHIVE

JR/1/278 **McIlhenny, Henry P.**
Glenveagh Castle, Churchill, Letterkenny, co. Donegal, Eire
1953-1979
Correspondence, also with estate staff, Lanning Roper, Sunningdale Nurseries, Mrs. McLafferty, Osborne & Co., Royal Moerheim Nurseries, and Messenger & Co. Ltd, bank statements, Ordnance Survey map, plant lists, sketches of buildings, grounds and views, and planting plans for gardens and grounds, including small formal garden, Belgian Walk, Italian garden and pleasure garden.
2 files; 1 roll; 1 plan folder

JR/1/279 **McClintock, David, editor, International Dendrology Society**
Braken Hill, Platt, Sevenoaks, Kent *1982-1990*
Correspondence.
1 file

JR/1/280 **McCorquadale, Mrs**
20 Ilchester Place, London *nd*
Planting plan for garden.
1 file; 1 roll

JR/1/281 **McGrath, Mrs**
No address given *1961*
Planting plan for rose garden.
1 file

JR/1/282 **Merton, John and Penelope**
Oare House, Oare, Wiltshire *1964*
Correspondence, plant list and planting plans for beds and garden.
1 file; 1 roll

JR/1/283 **Merry, Mrs Eion**
Glen Phoineas, Beauly, Inverness-shire, Scotland
nd 1950s
Planting plans for garden.
1 file; 1 roll

JAMES RUSSELL ARCHIVE

JR/1/284 **Middleton, Lord Michael and Lady Janet**
Birdsall House, Malton, North Yorkshire 1974-1975
Correspondence, plant lists and planting plan for garden.
1 file

JR/1/285 **Middlesex Hospital, London** 1961
Correspondence with Brig. G.P. Hardy Roberts, the secretary superintendent, plant list and planting plans. Also sketch view of Westminster Hospital.
1 file; 1 roll

JR/1/286 **McQuire, John F.**
Deer Dell, Botany Hill, The Sands, Farnham, Surrey
1985-1987
Correspondence.
1 file

JR/1/287 **McGuire, J.D.**
Emsworth and Newtown Park, Blackrock, co. Dublin, Ireland
1956-1957
Correspondence, plant lists and planting plans for gardens.
1 file; 1 roll

JR/1/288 **Miller-Mundy, Major Peter**
Sparsholt Manor, near Wantage, Berkshire 1958-1971
Correspondence, also with Sunningdale Nurseries, plant lists, section of Ordnance Survey map and planting plans.
1 file

JR/1/289 **Mills, Mrs C.B.**
17 Kensington Palace Gardens, London 1961-1962
Correspondence, also with Taylor & Marr Ltd, plant lists and planting plans for garden.
1 file; 1 roll

JR/1/290 **Monrovia Nursery Co.**
Azusa, California, USA 1972-1973
Correspondence, plant lists, invoices, delivery notes, credit balance slips, banking transfer forms.
1 file

James Russell Archive

JR/1/291 **Ministry of Agriculture: Export Charges** 1987-1992
Correspondence, information booklets and forms: 'Application for examination & certification of plants for export' and 'Application for export services'.
1 file

JR/1/292 **Ministry of Agriculture** 1979-1990
Correspondence, information booklets, plant lists, licences and forms: 'Soil testing for potato cyst eelworm (exports)', 'Exports - growing season inspection report', 'Notice of goods detained', 'Notice relating to the importation of plants and plant products carrying or infected with plant pests', 'phytosanitary certificate for plants and plant products', and 'Application for permission to import plants (nursery stock)'.
1 file

JR/1/293 **Mocatta, Mrs Pamela**
Carvers, Haslemere, Surrey nd
Planting plan for garden.
1 file; 1 roll

JR/1/294 **Monckton, Viscountess of Brenchley, Bridget**
6 King's Bench Walk, Temple, London and Folkington, Sussex
1964
Correspondence, plant list for garden.
1 file

JR/1/295 **Montague, Lord**
Beaulieu Palace House, Beaulieu, Hampshire 1978-1979
Correspondence, also with staff, building and planting plans.
1 file; 1 roll

JR/1/296 **More O'Ferrall, Roderic**
Kildangan, Monasterevan, co. Kildare, Eire 1971
Correspondence, plant list and planting plans for garden.
1 file

JR/1/297 **Morley, Derek and Marie-Josee**
The Quaives, Wickhambreaux, Kent 1958-1964
Correspondence, also with Sunningdale Nurseries, and plant lists.
1 file

JAMES RUSSELL ARCHIVE

JR/1/298 **Morley, Mr D. and Mrs M-J**
Islanmore, Croom, co. Limerick, Eire 1954-1955
Correspondence, also with Sunningdale Nurseries, plant lists and planting plans for garden.
1 file

JR/1/299 **Marriott, Richard**
Boynton Hall, Bridlington, Humberside 1981
Correspondence.
1 file

JR/1/300 **Mostyn-Owen, W.**
Aberuchill Castle, Comrie, Perthshire 1964-1965
Correspondence, plant list and planting plan for garden.
1 file; 1 roll

JR/1/301 **Mowbray & Stourton, Lady Jane and Lord Charles**
Marcus House, by Forfar, Angus, Scotland 1955-1971
Correspondence, Ordnance Survey map, plant lists and planting plans for garden.
1 file; 1 roll

JR/1/302 **Moulton-Barrett, Mrs**
The House of Glennie, by Huntly, Aberdeenshire, Scotland
1964-1965
Correspondence, plant lists and planting plans for walled garden and grounds.
1 file; 1 roll

JR/1/303 **Muir Smith, Mrs E.**
The White Cottage, Gracious Pond, Chobham, Surrey
1955
Ordnance Survey map, sketches of views, planting plans for garden.
1 file; 1 roll

James Russell Archive

JR/1/304 *Mulholland, the Hon. Mrs John*
Weston Marks, Upton Grey, near Basingstoke, Hampshire
1967
Correspondence, plant list and planting plans for garden.
1 file; 1 roll

JR/1/305 *Mountgarrett, Viscountess*
Staineley House, South Staineley, near Harrogate, Yorkshire
1970
Correspondence, also with Murrells of Shrewbury, and plant list.
1 file

JR/1/306 *Naylor Leyland, Sir Vivyan*
Nantclwyd Hall, Nantclwyd, Denbighshire, North Wales
1954-1965
Correspondence, also with staff, Sunningdale Nurseries, Hillier & Sons, quotations from A.F. Woodcock, The Barnham Nurseries Ltd and T. Hilling & Co. Ltd, plant lists and planting plans for rhododendron planting, garden and grounds.
1 file; 1 roll; 1 plan folder

JR/1/307 *Nevile, H.N.*
Aubourn Hall, Lincoln, Lincolnshire 1976
Correspondence, plant list and planting plans for garden.
1 file

JR/1/308 *Nevill, Lady Rupert*
Horstead Place, Uckfield, Sussex and Uckfield House, Sussex
1957-1978
Correspondence, also with Sunningdale Nurseries and Hunters Solicitors, plant lists and planting plans for garden.
1 file; 1 roll

JR/1/309 *Newman, Commander and Lady Joan*
Panfield Hall, Braintree, Essex 1964-1965
Correspondence, plant lists and planting plans for garden.
1 file; 1 roll

James Russell Archive

JR/1/310 **Nicholls, Mrs**
Brookfield House 1957
Planting plans for garden.
1 file; 1 roll

JR/1/311 **Norman, the Hon. Mrs Willoughby**
Pickwell Manor, Melton Mowbray, Leicestershire 1961
Planting pans for garden.
1 file; 1 roll

JR/1/312 **Norman, Capt. E.D. and Mrs**
The Yews, Coneysthorpe, North Yorkshire 1982-1983
Correspondence.
1 file

JR/1/313 **Northumberland, Duke and Duchess of**
Syon House, Isleworth, Middlesex 1952-1956
Correspondence, also with staff, Sunningdale Nurseries, plant lists and planting plans for greenhouse, shrub border and garden.
1 file; 1 roll

JR/1/314 **Norton, Mrs Vera**
The Manor House, Whalton, Morpeth, Northumberland
1967
Correspondence, plant list and planting plans for garden.
1 file; 1 roll

JR/1/315 **Nuttall, Sir Nicholas**
La Playa, Blue Hills, Lyford Clay, Nassau, Bahamas; Lowesby Hall, Leicestershire 1976-1987
Correspondence, also to the Festival Office at Malton, Anmore Exotics, Limberlost Nurseries, Read's Nursery, The Palm Centre, Honey Brothers Ltd, Dow Flora (Singapore) Pte Ltd, Foxhill Nursery, Giddy's Nursery with catalogue of cycad seedlings, Ministry of Agriculture, Marcel Lecoufle, Tropic Flora Co., Mrs Langlois, Hogg Robinson (UK) Ltd, American Express, Fred C. Galle, Charles Fernil, Ryedale Travel, Philip Jebb, travel documents and itinerary, plant lists, photographs, section of Ordnance Survey map, building and planting plans for gardens. Also an article 'The Retreat', from 'Currents', the Bahamas National Trust.
see also JR/1/458
2 files; 4 rolls

James Russell Archive

JR/1/316 **O'Keeffe, Paddy, producer**
Special Current Affairs, BBC, Broadcasting House, London
1981-1982
Correspondence, also re. 'Gardening at Brideshead' interview.
1 file

JR/1/317 **Ormiston, Alan and Ursula**
Holford House, North Chailey, Sussex 1960-1962
Correspondence and plant lists.
1 file

JR/1/318 **Orr-Ewing, Major Sir Ronald and Lady**
Cardross, Port of Menteith Station, Kippen, Stirlingshire
1962-1963
Correspondence, plant lists and planting plan.
1 file; 1 roll

JR/1/319 **Parkinson, Marjorie**
Wonersh House, Wonersh, near Guildford, Surrey
1964
Correspondence, Ordnance Survey map, plant list and planting plans for rose bed and garden.
1 file; 1 roll

JR/1/320 **Parkinson, Stuart**
The Elms, Bubwith, Selby, Yorkshire 1972
Correspondence, plant list and planting plan for garden.
1 file

JR/1/321 **Peech, Neil M. and Peggy**
Park House, Firbeck, near Worksop, Nottinghamshire and Steetley Company Ltd, PO Box No. 6, Worksop, Nottinghamshire (Gateford and Whitwell) 1961-1963
Correspondence, also with staff, plant lists and planting plans for gardens.
1 file; 1 roll

JAMES RUSSELL ARCHIVE

JR/1/322 **Pelly, E.**
Juniper Hill, Penn, Buckinghamshire nd
Plant list and planting plans.
1 file; 1 roll

JR/1/323 **Pending correspondence** 1979-1981
Correspondence with J. Younno, Daviaj Alan W. Lewis, Chestnut Lodge, Cobham, Surrey; G.L.G Noel of the NationalTrust and R.M. Chaplain.

JR/1/324 **Percy, Sir Richard and Lady Sarah**
Lesbury House, Alnwick, Northumberland 1966-1967
Correspondence, plant list and planting plans for garden.
1 file; 1 roll

JR/1/325 **Perkins, Mrs**
Plumpton Place 1987-1988
Correspondence, also with Tom Stewart-Smith, plant lists and planting plans for rose garden. Also photocopies of roses from Gertrude Jekyll book and lists of roses from 'Classic Roses', Peter Beales, and from book by G.S. Thomas.
1 file

JR/1/326 **Pilditch, Dennis and Joyce**
Bredfield Place, Woodbridge, Suffolk 1968-1970
Correspondence, plant lists and planting plan for garden.
1 file

JR/1/327 **Pinto, Mrs Gladys**
The Gothic House, Walmer, Kent 1965-1966
Correspondence and plant list.
1 file

JR/1/328 **Plant Centre**
Castle Howard, North Yorkshire 1984-1990
Correspondence, also with George Howard, Brian Hutchinson, Ian Duncan, Clearfast Ltd, Marks & Spencer Ltd, invoices with M.A.R. Cayzer, Firma C. Esveld, Sir. R. Storey, E. de Rothschild, Exbury Gardens Ltd, Glendoick Gardens Ltd, Croxden Compost Co., P. Chappell, Hergest Croft Gardens, Nippress Forwarding Ltd, export and

James Russell Archive

import forms, notes of Clifton Nurseries, Syon House, Wisley, Windsor, Sunningdale and Waterers of Bagshot, costing for establishing plant centre, plant lists, price list of EFG (Nurseries) Ltd for autumn 1978.
1 file

JR/1/329 **Plunkett, Col. Randall**
Dunsany Castle, co. Meath, Eire 1954-1958
Correspondence, also with staff, G.S. Thomas and Sunningdale Nurseries, Messrs John Black Ltd, London Airport, plant lists and planting plans for borders and garden.
1 file; 1 roll

JR/1/330 **Northern Police Convalescent Home**
St. Andrews, Harlow Moor Road, Harrogate, North Yorkshire
1986
Correspondence with superintendent, plant list, planting plans and plant tag.
1 file

JR/1/331 **Pollitzer, G.E.**
Rystwood House 1962
Planting plan for garden.
1 file

JR/1/332 **Porchester, Lord**
Milford Lake House, Burghclere, Newbury, Berkshire and 35 Cadogan Lane, London 1956-1982
Correspondence, also with staff, the Hon. G. Herbert, Tilhill Forestry Ltd, Sunningdale Nurseries, Knaphill Nursery Ltd, Hillier & Sons, H.W. Dean & Son, Fred. G. Meyer, Johns Inc., Sutton & Sons Ltd, Southern Growers, Telston Nurseries and F.G. Barcock & Co., invoices, plant tags, plant lists, building and planting plans for formal garden at Milford Lake House and gardens at both.
1 file; 1 roll

JR/1/333 **Price, D.E.C.**
Kilmokea House, Campile, via Waterford, co. Wexford, Eire
1961-1965
Correspondence, plant lists and planting plans for border and garden.
1 file; 1 roll

JAMES RUSSELL ARCHIVE

JR/1/334 **Priest, Jim and Sylvie**
Les Ecuries, Royaumont, Luzarches, France   1984-1992
Correspondence and plant list.
1 file

JR/1/335 **Priestman, Mrs**
Slaley Hall, Slaley near Hexham, Northumberland and Halkin Street, London   1953-1954
Correspondence, plant lists and planting plans for beds, terraces and garden at Slaley and garden at Halkin.
1 file; 1 roll

JR/1/336 **Profumo, Jack and Valerie**
The Dower House, Buntingford, Hertfordshire   1967-1974
Correspondence, also with Tilehurst Potteries, photographs, newspaper cuttings 'Are You Deprived by Lime?' by Fred Whitsey, plant list and planting plans for walled garden, white border and garden.
1 file

JR/1/337 **Pumfrey, Mrs J.A.**
Brampton Lodge, Torksey, Lincoln, Lincolnshire   1966-1968
Correspondence, plant lists and planting plans for garden.
1 file; 1 roll

JR/1/338 **Pumfrey, Paul and Marie-Therese**
The Lawns, Gainsborough, Lincolnshire and Moreton House, Gainsborough, Lincolnshire   1969-1970
Correspondence, plant list and planting plans for the garden.
1 file

JR/1/339 **Radcliffe, Capt. J.B.E.**
Rudding Park, Harrogate, Yorkshire   1953-1971
Correspondence, also with staff, Sunningdale Nurseries, statement of account, Lloyd's Bank Ltd, T. Hilling & Co. Ltd, J. Scott & Co., plant lists and planting plans for flower garden, walled garden and the garden.
1 file; 1 roll

JR/1/340 **Rainbird, George**
Old Rectory, Whichford and Whichford House, Shipston-on-Stour, Warwickshire 1955-1973
Correspondence, also with G.S. Thomas at Sunningdale Nurseries, invoices, plant lists and planting plans for gardens.
1 file; 1 roll

JR/1/341 **Read, Brigadier E.**
Pilgrims Way, Farnham, Surrey 1955-1957
Planting plans for garden.
1 file; 1 roll

JR/1/342 **Redditch Development Corporation**
Holmwood, Plymouth Road, Redditch, Worcestershire
1970-1976
Correspondence, also with Marcel Lecoufle, John Huggan & Co. Ltd, Sir Edward Thompson, Luwasa (Hydroculture) Ltd, promotional literature, invoices, minutes, plant lists, sketches of plants, building and planting plans.
JR/1/389
1 file

JR/1/343 **Reid, Lt. Col. J.W and Mrs**
Manor House Farm, Carlton Husthwaite, Thirsk, Yorkshire
1969
Correspondence, plant lists and planting plan for garden.
1 file

JR/1/344 **Royal Horticultural Society (Chris Brickell)** 1970-1988
Correspondence, also with A.J. Halstead, Barry Ambrose, Eddie de Rothschild, Mr. Arai, John Sanders, Duncan Donald, K.M. Harris, Audrey V. Brooks, J.R. Cutler, A.C. Leslie, G. Pycraft, J Paclt, Russell H. Coates, J.R. Connell. Also bulletin no. 39 of the Rhododendron and Camellia Group, agenda for SGM 1987, book lists, plant lists, reports: 'Biological Control of Glasshouse Pests', 'Frankfurt International Book Fair 12-17 October 1983', 'Yuccas in Britain'.
1 file

JAMES RUSSELL ARCHIVE

JR/1/345 **Richardson, Col. F.**
Greenfields nd
Planting plans for garden.
1 file; 1 roll

JR/1/346 **Riley-Smith, Mrs T.A.**
Isle of Jura, Scotland and Inholmes, Tadcaster, Yorkshire
1961-1965
Correspondence, Ordnance Survey maps, plant lists and planting plans for rose garden, water garden and grounds.
1 file; 1 roll

JR/1/347 **Rochford, Thomas Rochford & Sons Ltd**
Turnford Hall Nurseries, Turnford, Broxbourne, Hertfordshire
1972
Correspondence, invoices and plant list.
1 file

JR/1/348 **Rootes, T.D.**
The Barn House, Alkerton, near Banbury, Warwickshire
1965-1967
Correspondence, also with Obby Waller, photograph, Ordnance Survey map, plant lists and building and planting plans for garden.
1 file; 1 roll

JR/1/349 **Rose, Lt. Col. A.J.C. and Mrs M.**
The Garden House, Dunira, Comrie, Perthshire, Scotland
1956-1965
Correspondence, plant lists and planting plans for garden.
1 file; 1 roll

JR/1/350 **Rotherwick, Dowager Lady**
Wallhurst Manor, Cowfold, Sussex nd
Planting plans for borders, terrace, walled garden and grounds.
JR/1/83
1 file; 1 roll

James Russell Archive

JR/1/351 ***Rothermere, Viscount***
Daylesford House, Moreton-in-Marsh, Gloucestershire
1962-1965
Correspondence, also with staff, John Thornton, Franklin & Jones, Ordnance Survey map, sketch of orangery, plant lists and planting plans for picking border, lakeside planting and orangery.
1 file; 1 roll

JR/1/352 ***Rotherwick, Lord***
Bletchingdon Park, Bletchingdon, Oxfordshire and Lanfine, Newmilns, Ayrshire, Scotland *1956-1963*
Correspondence, also with staff, Sunningdale Nurseries, Ordnance Survey map, plant lists and planting plans for gardens.
1 file; 1 roll

JR/1/353 ***Rothamstead Experimental Station***
Harpenden, Hertfordshire *1985*
Correspondence with Ailwyn de Ramsey, Prof. E.A. Bell, Sir William Henderson, Duke of Northumberland, Ainsworth Evans Partnership, Sir Leslie Fowden, plant lists and planting plans for water garden and grounds.
1 file

JR/1/354 ***Sacher, Mrs Michael***
18 Phillimore Gardens, London *1961*
Planting plan for orangery.
1 file; 1 roll

JR/1/355 ***Salisbury, Machioness of***
The Manor House, Cranborne, Dorset *1972*
Correspondence, also with staff.
1 file

JR/1/356 ***Sandars, Mr J.E. and Mrs M.***
Great Burton Hall, Gainsborough, Lincolnshire
1960-1967
Correspondence, Ordnance Survey map, plant lists and planting plans for borders, rhododendron planting and garden.
1 file; 1 roll

JAMES RUSSELL ARCHIVE

JR/1/357 **Sandringham**
The Estate Office, Sandringham, Norfolk   1983-1984
Correspondence with agent, Julian Loyd, and notes on plants.
1 file

JR/1/358 **Saudi Arabia**   1978-1979
Correspondence with OAD (Agriculture) Ltd UK office, and planting plans for window boxes.
1 file

JR/1/359 **Scarbrough, Earl of**
Sandbeck Park, Rotherham, Yorkshire   1970-1978
Correspondence, also with Royal Horticultural Society, G.S. Thomas, Nigel Nicholson and Nigel Broackes.
1 file

JR/1/360 **Scheunert, Col. Kot and Ruth**
Inish Rath, Linaskea, Northern Ireland   1954-1967
Correspondence, also with staff, Mrs M. Kennedy, G.S. Thomas and Sunningdale Nurseries, Ordnance Survey map, plant lists and planting plans for garden.
1 file; 1 roll

JR/1/361 **Schollick, Very Revd Canon**
Wardley Hall, Worsley, Manchester, Lancashire   1960-1962
Correspondence and planting plans for garden.
1 file; 1 roll

JR/1/362 **Scott**
Abu Dhabi   1977
Correspondence with Smith & Norwood and Arup Associates, plant lists and planting plans for conservatory.
1 file

JR/1/363 **Sharples, Mrs**
Southfield Farm, Chawton, Hampshire   1957
Planting plans for border and garden.
1 file; 1 roll

JAMES RUSSELL ARCHIVE

JR/1/364 ***Shawcross, Lady***
Friston Place, Sussex   1962-1967
Correspondence, Ordnance Survey map, plant lists and planting plans for tree planting and garden.
1 file; 1 roll

JR/1/365 ***Shell Gardens***
George Rainbird Ltd,   1962
Correspondence with George Rainbird Ltd, John Wolfers, the National Trust for Scotland, Newby Hall Estate, Percy Hennell, Rudding Park, Belvoir Estates Ltd, Castle Howard, RHS Wisley, G.S. Thomas, Haddon Hall, Sissinghurst Castle, Windsor Great Park re. Shell Gardens Scheme.
1 file

JR/1/366 ***Siddeley Landscapes, the Hon. Randle Siddeley***
36 Bear Lane, London   1978-1979
Correspondence, plant lists and planting plans for Mortimer House and 'Jardin d'hiver' by Provenence Jardins.
1 file

JR/1/367 ***Sitwell, Sacheverell, Georgia, Francis***
Weston Hall, Towcester, Northamptonshire   1959-1979
Correspondence, also with John Waterer & Sons & Crisp Ltd and others, plant lists, sketches and planting plans for garden.
1 file; 1 roll

JR/1/368 ***Smith, Ian***
Walton Hall   1956
Planting plans for garden.
1 file; 1 roll

JR/1/369 ***Smith, Mrs***
Laguna, Murthly, Perthshire, Scotland   1966
Correspondence and plant list.
1 file

James Russell Archive

JR/1/370 **Speke, Col. N.H.R. and Mrs A.**
Shawell House, Corbridge, Northumberland, and Aydon White House, Corbridge, Northumberland 1952-1962
Correspondence, plant lists and planting plans for gardens.
1 file

JR/1/371 **Starr, Keith**
Keith Starr Alpines (County Park), County Park Nursery, Essex Gardens, Hornchurch, Essex 1981
Correspondence.
1 file

JR/1/372 **Stevenson, Mrs. Rosa**
Tower Court, Ascot, Berkshire 1951-1960
Correspondence, also with Sunningdale, Col. Edwards and Starthern & Blair, statement of account and plant lists.
1 file

JR/1/373 **Stevens, Mrs Jocelyn**
Testbourne, Long Parish, near Andover, Hampshire
1975
Correspondence and plant list.
1 file

JR/1/374 **Stewart, Major John**
Ardvorlich, Lochearnhead, Perthshire, Scotland
1956
Correspondence, plant list and planting plans for herbaceous border and garden.
1 file; 1 roll

JR/1/375 **Stewart-Smith, Mrs Pamela**
South Park Farm, South Godstone, Surrey 1966-1967
Correspondence and plant lists.
1 file; 1 roll

JR/1/376 **Stewart, Mrs**
Barclay 1956
Planting plan for garden.
1 file; 1 roll

JAMES RUSSELL ARCHIVE

JR/1/377 **Storey, Sir Richard and Virginia**
Settrington House, Malton, North Yorkshire 1979-1991
Correspondence, also with staff, Francis F. Johnson & Partners, R.F. Wood General Manager (Sunderland) Echo, Messrs Smiths Gore, Askham Bryan College, plant lists, section of Ordnance Survey map and planting plans for Dipper Wood, the Low Garden and grounds.
1 file; 1 roll

JR/1/378 **Stormont House, Belfast, Northern Ireland** 1956-1962
Correspondence with W.H. Hamill and others at the Ministries of Finance and Agriculture, Northern Ireland, Slieve Donard Nurseries, and Viscountess Brookeborough, plant lists and planting plans.
3 files; 1 roll; 1 plan folder

JR/1/379 **Stuart-Black, I.H.**
The Old Manse, Balfron, Stirlingshire, Scotland
nd
Planting plans for border and grounds.
1 file

JR/1/380 **Stuart-Black, Major A.A.**
Highfield Park, Heckfield, Basingstoke, Hampshire
1954
Correspondence, plant lists and planting plan for borders and garden.
1 file

JR/1/381 **Sunningdale Nurseries Ltd**
Nursery and Garden Centre, Windlesham, Surrey
1952-1979
Correspondence with K. Beeson, E. King and other staff of Sunningdale Nurseries, Dobbie & Co. Ltd, C.W.J. Ballard, C.H. Pennington of Waterers Nurseries and Garden Centres, M. Foster, Mrs. Hanbury Williams, John Profumo and N.G. Broackes, and invoices, statements and plant lists. Plans for torchere and mermaid pool. Planting plans for rose and shrub border and for nursery grounds. Sketches of tubs, pots, urns, bowls, vases and other containers. Ordnance Survey maps.
2 files; 1 roll; 2 plan folders

JAMES RUSSELL ARCHIVE

JR/1/382 **Swedish Burial Ground**
Brookwood Cemetery, Surrey nd
Planting plan.
1 file; 1 roll

JR/1/383 **Talbot, the Hon. Mrs [T.G.]**
Falconhurst, Edenbridge, Kent nd
Ordnance Survey map of Kent and Sussex.
1 file

JR/1/384 **Taylor, Mrs Jane**
Harker-Taylor Services, The Level, Pillowell, Lydney, Gloucestershire and National Council for the Conservation of Plants and Gardens 1980-1986
Correspondence and catalogues.
1 file

JR/1/385 **Taylour, Robert S.**
Wycliffe Hall, Barnard Castle, co. Durham 1985-1989
Correspondence, also with Richard Newbury of Crowther of Syon Lodge, Francis F. Johnson & Partners, Messrs Smiths Gore, Halls Home & Gardens, Traditional Trellis, particulars of property, plant lists, bank statement, section of Ordnance Survey map and planting plans for garden.
1 file

JR/1/386 **Terry, N.G.**
Goddards, 27 Tadcaster Road, Dringhouses, York 1978
Correspondence also with George W. Smith.
1 file

JR/1/387 **Thomas, Peter**
Currarevach, Chase Lane, Haslemere, Surrey and Warren Cottage, Haslemere, Surrey 1966-1984
Correspondence, quotations and plant lists.
1 file; 1 roll

JAMES RUSSELL ARCHIVE

JR/1/388 **Cricket St. Thomas (Wildlife & Leisure Park)**
The West Country Wildlife Park, Chard, Somerset
1982-1988
Correspondence with W.J.D Taylor, expenses, plant lists and planting plans.
1 file

JR/1/389 **Thompson, Sir Edward**
Gatacre Park, Bridgnorth, Shropshire   1971-1972
Correspondence, plant list and planting plans for rose garden, beds and garden.
see also JR/1/342
1 file

JR/1/390 **Towneley, Simon**
Dyneley, Burnley, Lancashire   1961-1986
Correspondence, Ordnance Survey map, plant lists and planting plans for ornamental beds and garden.
1 file; 1 roll

JR/1/391 **Ropner, Lady Auriol**
Bryngwyn, Bwich-y-Cibau, Llanfyllin, Powys
1981-1991
Correspondence, also with R.A. Watson of Thorp Perrow Arboretum, Bedale, North Yorkshire, John Beach of Park House, Bedale, North Yorkshire, and information about the Hon. Mrs Geddes.
1 file

JR/1/392 **Trevor-Roper, Lady Alexandria**
Chiefswood, Melrose, Roxburghshire, Scotland and 8 St. Aldates, Oxford, Oxfordshire   1966
Correspondence.
1 file

JAMES RUSSELL ARCHIVE

JR/1/393 **Trustees of the Fellowes Trust**
Tree Planting Scheme, Abbots Ripton Estate, Cambridgeshire
1976-1978
Correspondence with Lord de Ramsey, J.F.E. Marks, William Duff & Son (Forfar) Ltd, N.H. Hyde of the Countryside Commission, J.R. Megginson, County Planning Office, summary of costs, catalogue, section of Ordnance Survey map, plant lists and planting plans.
1 file

JR/1/394 **Tufnell, Major Timothy**
The Dower House, Old Windsor, Berkshire 1971-1973
Correspondence, also with Stewards (Ferndown) Nurseries Ltd, invoices, plant lists and planting plans for garden.
1 file

JR/1/395 **Tusting, John C.**
Braehead, Carlton 1955
Planting plans for herbaceous border and garden.
1 file; 1 roll; 1 plan folder

JR/1/396 **Unprinted Catalogue** 1975-1976
Correspondence with Helen Hubble, Peter Bates, Michael Wright, order for Messrs Thomas Rochford & Sons Ltd, plant lists and draft catalogue for Exotic Plants.
1 file

JR/1/397 **Upcher, T.**
Sheringham Hall, Norfolk 1956
Planting plan of azalea border.
1 file; 1 roll

JR/1/398 **Van Oss, O.**
Weston 1962
Planting plan for garden at 'Weston'.
Van Oss was headmaster at Charterhouse.
1 file; 1 roll

JR/1/399 **Vandervell, Mrs**
Barntiles, Blackhills, Esher, Surrey   1955
Planting plans for garden.
1 file; 1 roll

JR/1/400 **Van Tubergen**
Koninklijke Bloembollen - en Zaadhan del van Tubergen BV,
Zwanenburg Nurseries, Haarlem, Holland   1972-1983
Correspondence, also with Copex Ltd, C.R. Armfield (Hull) Ltd, orders, confirmations and invoices, mail transfer advice forms re. payments and catalogues.
1 file

JR/1/401 **Vaughan, Viscountess**
35 Loundon Road   1955
Planting plan for garden.
1 file; 1 roll

JR/1/402 **Verulam, Earl of**
Gorhambury House, St. Albans, Hertfordshire 1973
Correspondence, plant lists, section of Ordnance Survey map and planting plan for garden.
1 file

JR/1/403 **Versepuy,**
International Versepuy, Tree Seeds Bank, 43 Lepuy, France
                                                 1980
Correspondence and insurance certificate.
1 file

JR/1/404 **Wagg, Jeremy**
Fordel, Glenfarg, Perthshire, Scotland   1972
Correspondence and plant lists.
1 file

JR/1/405 **Walker, Major Patrick and Mrs S.M.**
Stones Place, Lincoln   1957-1959
Correspondence and plant lists.
1 file

James Russell Archive

JR/1/406 **Walker, Mr Ronald A. and Mrs N.**
The Cottage, Bawtrey, Yorkshire 1965-1966
Correspondence, plant list and planting plan for garden.
1 file; 1 roll

JR/1/407 **Walker Munro, Michael**
Hurdcott House, Barford St. Martin, Salisbury, Wiltshire
 1962
Correspondence, Ordnance Survey map, plant list and planting plans for terrace garden and grounds.
1 file; 2 rolls

JR/1/408 **Walsh, Lady Helen**
Pigeon House, Frampton, Dorchester, Dorset 1961-1966
Correspondence, Ordnance Survey map, plant lists and planting plan for garden.
1 file; 1 roll

JR/1/409 **Ward, Viscountess of Witley formerly Lady Barbara Astor**
Friars Well, Aynho, near Banbury, Oxfordshire
 1961-1963
Correspondence, plant lists and planting plans for magnolia garden, formal garden and grounds.
1 file; 1 roll

JR/1/410 **Warlow-Harry, Mrs**
Westfield Farm, Moreton Morrell, Warwickshire
 1963-1964
Correspondence, plant list and planting plans for garden.
1 file; 1 roll

JR/1/411 **Warren, Nigel**
Compton Bishop, Somerset 1959-1961
Correspondence, photograph, plant lists, building and planting plans for rose garden and grounds.
1 file

James Russell Archive

JR/1/412 **Watkins, Mrs Daphne**
Egbury House, St. Mary Bourne, Andover, Hampshire
1961-1963

Correspondence, plant lists and planting plans for long border and garden.
1 file; 1 roll

JR/1/413 **Watson, Mrs Katherine**
Watson's Bookshop, The Hill, Burford, Oxfordshire
1980

Correspondence.
1 file

JR/1/414 **Watt, Alistair**
Otway Ridge Arboretum, Lavers Hill, Victoria, Australia
1989-1992

Correspondence and seed and plant lists.
1 file

JR/1/415 **Wedgwood, the Hon. Josiah**
Josiah Wedgwood & Sons Ltd, Barlaston, Stoke on Trent, Staffordshire
1952-1953

Correspondence with Messrs Josiah Wedgwood & Sons Ltd, Josiah Wedgwood, and staff, David Higgins, Sutton & Sons Ltd and Sunningdale Nurseries, expenses sheet, list of gardeners, plant lists and planting plans for plantations and grounds.
1 file; 1 roll

JR/1/416 **Weir, James and Mora**
Skeldon House, Dalrymple, Ayrshire, Scotland
1954-1966

Correspondence, also with staff and Sunningdale Nurseries, Ordnance Survey maps, plant lists, sketches of rose supports, and planting plans for garden.
1 file; 1 roll; 1 plan folder

James Russell Archive

JR/1/417 ***Weldon, Sir Anthony***
Rathdonnell, Trentagh, co. Donegal, Eire   1953-1962
Correspondence, also with John German & Son, Sunningdale Nurseries, Messrs Gander & White Ltd, Lt. Col. J.D.C. Brownlow, British Transport Commission, Caulfields Ltd and Lionel Perry, plant lists, sketch of view and planting plan for garden.
1 file

JR/1/418 ***Wemyss & March, Earl of and Lady***
Gosford House, Longniddry, East Lothian, Scotland
    1951-1953
Correspondence, also with staff and Sunningdale Nurseries, plant lists and planting plans for garden.
1 file; 1 roll

JR/1/419 ***Wernher, Lady Zia***
Luton Hoo, Luton, Bedfordshire   nd
Planting plans for herbaceous border, azaleas and garden.
1 file

JR/1/420 ***West, Lady***
Claxton Hall, Claxton, Yorkshire   1960
Correspondence, plant list and planting plan for borders.
1 file; 1 roll

JR/1/421 ***West, James and Camilla***
Alscot Park, Stratford-upon-Avon, Warwickshire
    1960-1968
Correspondence, Ordnance Survey map, plant lists, sketches of views and planting plans for formal garden, garden and grounds.
1 file; 1 roll

JR/1/422 ***Westminster, Duchess of, Sally***
Eaton Hall, Chester, Cheshire; Saighton Grange, Chester, Cheshire   1964-1990
Correspondence, also with Bobby, Loelia Duchess of Westminster, and staff, plant lists and planting plans for Eaton 'Puddings', rose beds and garden.
1 file; 1 roll

James Russell Archive

JR/1/423 **Westminster, Duchess of, Viola**
Eaton Hall, Chester, Cheshire 1969-1970
Correspondence and plant list.
1 file

JR/1/424 **Westminster, Duchess of, Loelia**
The Old Vicarage, Send, near Woking, Surrey nd
Building plan for terrace, by Sir Martyn Beckett.
1 file

JR/1/425 **Whitmee, Mr Brian A.C. and Tweets**
Barry Lodge, Kintbury, Newbury, Berkshire 1981-1982
Correspondence, also with Peter Beales.
1 file

JR/1/426 **Whitmee, Mr Brian A.C. and Tweets**
Bolney Lodge, Bolney, Sussex 1968-1973
Correspondence, plant lists and planting plans for garden.
1 file

JR/1/427 **Whitsey, Fred**
Avens Mead, 20 Oast Road, Oxted, Surrey 1973-1988
Correspondence, also with Tony Venison of Country Life.
1 file

JR/1/428 **Whittaker, Mrs**
The Land of Nod, Neadley, Bordon, Hampshire
 nd
Planting plans for garden.
1 file

JR/1/429 **Willis, Peggy, Mrs Victor, formerly Mrs Thomas Dunne**
Ivy Lodge, Radway, Warwickshire and Chadshunt, Kineton, Warwickshire 1954-1989
Correspondence, also with staff, Capt. Thomas Dunne, and Sunningdale Nurseries, sketches of garden, plant lists and building and planting plans for the Folly, rose borders, and garden.
1 file; 2 rolls

James Russell Archive

JR/1/430 **Wills, the Hon. Patrick**
Lichfield Downs, Whitchurch, Hampshire   1964-1966
Correspondence, plant list and planting plans for garden.
1 file; 1 roll

JR/1/431 **Wilton, Earl of**
Ramsbury Manor, Marlborough, Wiltshire   1953-1956
Correspondence, also with staff, Messrs John German & Son, and Sunningdale Nurseries, plant lists and planting plans for borders and garden.
1 file; 1 roll

JR/1/432 **Winch, Mrs**
Castle Cary, Guernsey, the Channel Isles   1958
Planting plans for grounds.
1 file; 1 roll

JR/1/433 **Wine**   1980-1981
Catalogue for Malmaison Wine Club and price lists for Australian Wine Centre.
1 file

JR/1/434 **Wingfield, Charles J.**
Bicton Heath House, Shrewsbury, Shropshire   1953-1954
Correspondence and plant list for garden.
1 file

JR/1/435 **Wingfield, Charles J.**
Onslow Hall, Bicton Heath, Shrewsbury, Shropshire
   1961-1962
Correspondence, plant lists and planting plans for terrace beds and garden.
1 file; 1 roll

JR/1/436 **Winn, G. Mark D.**
Aldby Park, Stamford Bridge, Yorkshire   1971-1973
Correspondence, plant lists, section of Ordnance Survey map and planting plan for garden.
1 file

JAMES RUSSELL ARCHIVE

JR/1/437 **Wombwell, V. Malcolm and Beryl**
Newburgh Priory, Coxwold, Yorkshire 1970-1971
Correspondence, acknowledgment slip from Murrells of Shrewsbury, plant lists and plan of rose border.
1 file

JR/1/438 **Wood, Michael**
Upton Grey Place, near Basingstoke, Hampshire and Churchmead, Upton Grey, near Basingstoke, Hampshire
1964-1967
Correspondence, also with V. Russell Smith and John Waterer Sons & Crisp Ltd, plant lists and building and planting plans for borders and gardens.
1 file; 1 roll

JR/1/439 **Worsley, Sir W. Marcus J.**
Hovingham Hall, Hovingham, Yorkshire 1975-1989
Correspondence, plant list and planting plans for wild garden, shrub border and gardens.
1 file

JR/1/440 **Worsley, Penelope and Oliver.**
Bolton Hall, Wilberfoss, Yorkshire 1970
Correspondence, plant list and planting plans for garden.
1 file

JR/1/441 **Wrightson, Sir John**
Neasham Hall, Darlington, Durham 1972
Correspondence, plant list and planting plans for rose beds and garden.
1 file

JR/1/442 **Wimborne, Viscountess Venetia**
Fontaine l'Abbe, Serquigny, Normandy, France 1989-1992
Correspondence, also with staff, Keith Anderson, Mill Lane Nursery, Mons. Michel Lebreton, David West, Peter Beales, Bambouseraie de Prefrance, Firma C. Esveld, Guy Watt, P. Chappell, Glook Export Services, Diana Mancroft, Exbury Trees Ltd, Pieter Zwijnenberg Junior, Henri Mestrallet of Week-End Service and others, travel and shipping documents, receipts, invoices, phytosanitary certificate, plant lists and planting plans for garden.
1 file

JR/1/443 **Waterers**   1968-1970
Correspondence with A.J. Young and H.R. Diamond of Imperial Chemical Industries Ltd, Jeremy James, G.H. Paul, Mrs. Bradstock, Charles Brocklehurst, David A. Keith, Mrs. O. Lancaster, Mr. Keely, Hon. A. Cayzer, M. Colvin, Countess of Lietrim, S. Aston, Capt. P. Lambert, Major W.A. Fife, J.W. Cameron of Lion Brewery - Hartlepool, Mr Bulman, Angela Wykeham, David Barnes, M.F. Fane, F. Dorrn, R.F. Rothwell, M.K. Irving, T.D. Higgins of John Waterers Sons & Crips Ltd, E. King of Sunningdale Nurseries. Correspondence concerns clients' gardens and the acquisition of Sunningdale Nurseries by Waterers. Plant lists, plant orders, invoices, expenses, financial and business arrangements with Waterers,
1 file

JR/1/444 **Younger, Mrs**
Craignish Castle, Ardfern, Argyllshire, Scotland
                                                   1959-1961
Correspondence, Ordnance Survey maps, plant lists and planting plans for garden.
1 file; 1 roll

JR/1/445 **Yorke, Mrs Susie**
Hull Foot, Worston, Clitheroe, Lancashire   1972
Correspondence, plant list and planting plans for garden.
1 file

JR/1/446 **Yugoslavia, plant lists**   1983-1985
Plant lists 'Hortus Botanicus Universitatis Skopiensis; Supplimentum ad delectum seminum 1983', 'Hortus Botanicus Universitatis Skopiensis Yugoslavia Delectus Seminum Sporarum Plantarumque Horti Botanici Universitatis Skopiensis' 1983, and 'Index Seminam, January 1985, Seeds Collected in the Wild' of the Washington Park Arboretum. Correspondence with Univerzitet Kirilli Metodii, Violoski Fabultet, Botanicka Gradina, Pastfach 1191 YU-91000, Skopje, Yugoslavia.
1 file

James Russell Archive

JR/1/447 ***Zetland, Marchioness of***
Aske, Richmond, Yorkshire nd
Planting plans for herbaceous and rose borders.
1 file; 1 roll

JR/1/448 ***Small Foreign Orders*** 1976-1977
Correspondence with Duncan & Davies Ltd of New Plymouth, New Zealand, Australian Plants Centre of Coombabah, Australia, B. Wall of Weybridge, Surrey, expenses and plant list.
1 file

JR/1/449 ***Tropic Flora***
51 & 79 Dunearn Road, Floral Mile, Singapore and 177 Changi Road, Singapore nd
Correspondence, also with Cynthia Grady of South Africa, Dow Flora (Singapore) Ltd, and plant lists.
1 file

JR/1/450 ***Rhododendron: Royal Botanic Garden, Kew, Surrey***
1978-1987
Correspondence with Patricia Ives, Brian Halliwell, Lynn Knight, Charlie M. Erskine, S. Andrews, Prof. J.K. Treharne, Anthony D. Schilling, J.L.S. Kessing, R. Ian Beyer, John B. Simmons, Hans J. Fleigner, at RBG, Kew. Also correspondence with Drs Fu Yenfeng, Chen Weilin and Jia Zhenghou of Institute of Botony, Academia Sinica Matthew Biggs, Laura Ponsonby .
RBG, Kew surplus seed, seedling, shrubs and tree lists for June 1986, July 1982, March 1982, December 1980, surplus fagaceae seedlings July 1982 and surplus seedlings from Korean expedition. Plant and collecting lists and notes.
Plant lists: 'List of Chinese Herbarium Specimens from Fan Jiu Shan' July 1986, 'Collection of Malus Species and Cultivars' at Long Ashton, 'Rhododendrons added to the collection 1978'.
Publications: 'The History and Development of the Arboretum at the Royal Botanic Gardens, Kew', 'The Plant World of Roberto Burle Marx, A Tour Presented by the Royal Botanic Gardens, Kew', and a copy of 'Vireya Vine'.
Plan of 'Royal Botanic Kew Living Collections Division'.
1 file

James Russell Archive

JR/1/451 Rhododendrons: Great Park, Windsor   1978-1987
Correspondence with John D. Bond, Mr Wiseman, Jocelyn James of Windsor and D. Bannister, I.M.C. Sheffield, and Roy Lancaster.
Catalogues and plant lists for stock spring and autumn 1987, autumn 1986, spring 1985, autumn 1984, 1983-1984, spring 1983, 1982-1983, 1981-1982. Other plant lists including 'Seedlings from National Arboretum of Washington's trip to Japan' and 'Wild collected seed from M & C Middleton, The Boat House, Potters Lane, Samlesbury, Preston'.
1 file

JR/1/452 Rhododendrons: Inventories, Lists etc.   1978-1981
'1981 Inventory', '1978 Inventory' and 'Rhododendrons added to the collection 1978'.
Orders, acknowledgements and correspondence with Glendoick Gardens Ltd, Exbury Gardens Ltd, Hydon Nurseries Ltd, Ming Park Close Estates, G. Reuthe Ltd, Foxhill Nurseries.
Correspondence with Mary Hall, secretary of Rhododendron Group, Harlow Car.
Copy of 'Rhododendrons in the British Isles - An Irreverent Approach' by D.E. Mayers.
1 file

JR/1/453 Rhododendrons: Royal Botanic Gardens, Wakehurst Place, Sussex   1978-1987
Correspondence with Anthony D. Schilling, Mr Lonsdale and report with plans for 'Proposed Sub-Tropical Garden Development Wakehurst Place'.
Plant despatch request forms, 1986, 1985, 1984 and plant lists.
Copy of notes re. R. fastigiatum from 'Notes from the RBG Edinburgh', vol 34, no. 1, 1975 and 'Report on a visit to the People's Republic of China' May-June 1978 by Peter S. Green and John B. Simmons.
1 file; 1 roll

JR/1/454 le Rougetel   1981-1989
Correspondence, also with Mr Chang Qing of Contemporary International Relations in Beijing and of Beijing Rose Society.
1 file

James Russell Archive

JR/1/455 ***Ponsonby, Laura***
17 South End, London   1981-1991
Correspondence.
1 file

JR/1/456 ***de Ramsey, Ailwyn***
Abbots Ripton Hall, Huntingdonshire   1976-1988
Correspondence, also with staff, including J.F.E. Marks, and with Mons. Lecoufle, Laura Ponsonby, Michael Gibson and others, photograph of spiraea, plant lists and newspaper cuttings.
see also JR/1/130
1 file

JR/1/457 ***Mason, Maurice***
Talbot Manor, Fincham, Kings Lynn, Norfolk   1972-1985
Correspondence, also with P.P. Markwell of Quaymount Ltd, Mr Bomer, Mons. Durand of Arboretum des Barres, P.G.E. Smallcombe of RBG Kew, J.D. Bond of the Great Park, Windsor, George Wortley Ltd, Mr Robinson re. Hillier Arboretum, and others, field notes from Mexico expedition 1984 and plant lists.
1 file

JR/1/458 ***Worswick, Albert E.***
Nassau, Bahamas   1985-1986
Planting plans for Templepan Wood and general layout of property.
see also JR/1/315
1 roll

JR/1/459 ***Castle Howard, Yorkshire***   1957
Planting plans for Ray Wood, the Arboretum, gardens and grounds at Castle Howard.
see also JR/1/264
1 roll

JR/1/460 ***Maryland***   nd
Planting plan for garden at Maryland.
1 plan

JAMES RUSSELL ARCHIVE

JR/1/461 **Wormald, Captain R.**
The Old Vicarage, Foston, Yorkshire nd
Planting plans for garden.
1 file

JR/1/462 **Sherriff, Mrs**
Ascreavie, Kingoldrum, Forfarshire, Scotland 1955
Planting plan for garden.
1 plan

JR/1/463 **Speight, Mr** 1957
Planting plan for garden.
1 file

JR/1/464 **Smiley**
Castle Frazer, Aberdeenshire nd
Ordnance Survey plan and planting plans for garden.
1 plan; 1 roll

JR/1/465 **Pope, Mrs**
Upton Grove, Tetbury, Gloucestershire 1955
Planting plan for garden.
1 plan; 1 roll

JR/1/466 **Macbeath, Mr J.** nd
Planting plan for rhododendrons and azaleas.
1 plan; 1 roll

JR/1/467 **Gaskell, Mr R.W.**
Gillow Manor, Harewood End, Herefordshire nd
Planting plan for garden.
1 plan; 1 roll

JR/1/468 **Carr, Mrs** nd
Planting plan for garden.
1 plan; 1 roll

JR/1/469 **Datchet Border, Windsor, Berkshire** nd
Planting plans for Datchet Border.
1 file; 1 roll

James Russell Archive

JR/1/470 **Riyadh, Saudi Arabia** 1980
Planting plans for 'Riyadh's World of Pleasure'.
1 file; 1 roll

JR/1/471 **No. 26 The Boltons** nd
Planting plan for garden
1 map In roll

JR/1/472 **Widcombe Manor, Somerset** nd
Ordnance Survey map and planting plan for garden.
2 maps in roll

JR/1/473 **Sezincote, Gloucestershire** nd
Ordnance Survey map of area.
1 map in roll

JR/2 PRINTED MATERIAL

JR/2/1 *Sale catalogue of James Russell's library.*

JR/2/2 *Personal bookplate of James Russell.*

INDEX OF PLACES AND PEOPLE

References are given to the list number not to page, except for roman numerals which refer to page numbers in the introduction. Businesses and companies are indexed by initial letter of the first name. Counties are given where possible, and countries for places abroad.

A.C. Rentaplant 1/171
Abbots Ripton Estate (Hunts) xix; 1/2/2; 1/393
— Hall (Hunts) 1/130; 1/456
Abe, Hisayori 1/224
Aberclovey (Mer) 1/17
Aberconway, Lady 1/2
Abergavenny, Marquis of xvi; 1/3
Aberuchill Castle (Perth) 1/300
Able-Smith, Mr, iv
— Mrs xvi; 1/1
Abu Dhabi vii
Achamore House (Argyll) 1/192
Achnacarry (Invern) 1/179
Adair, Maj. Gen. Sir A. 1/4
Adderley, S. 1/138
Ainsworth Evans Partnership 1/353
Airlie Castle (Angus) 1/5
Airlie, Countess of 1/5
— Earl of 1/5
Aldby Park (Yorks) 1/436
Aldermaston (Berks) 1/222
Aldworth (Berks) 1/241
Alfred Holt and Co. Ltd. 1/189
Alkerton, The Barn House 1/348
Allanbank (Berwick) 1/27
Alnwick (N'land) 1/324
Alscot Park (Warks) 1/421
Alston, N. 1/6
Ambrose, Barry 1/344
American Express 1/315
Ampfield (Hants) 1/181; 1/199
Anderson, Keith 1/442
Andover (Hants) 1/59; 1/373; 1/412
Andrews, S. 1/450
Anmer Hall (Norf) 1/228
Anmore Exotics 1/315
Annbark (Ayr) 1/261
Anson, Mrs G.H. 1/7
Arai, Mr 1/344
— Minoru 1/224
Ardfern (Argyll) 1/444
Ardvolich (Perth) 1/374
Arimasa, Hiroyuki 1/224
Arisaka, Satoshi 1/224
Arley Hall (Ches) 1/10

Arthur, Mrs E. 1/9
Arup Associates x; 1/18; 1/19; 1/20; 1/21; 1/22, 1/23, 1/24, 1/225, 1/362
Ascot (Berks) 1/26; 1/372
— Place (Berks) 1/26
— Racecourse (Berks) 1/14
— South (Berks) 1/78
Ascott (Beds) 1/25
Ascreavie (Forfar) 1/462
Asdale (Surrey) 1/271
Ashbridge Arboretum 1/172
Ashbrook, Viscountess 1/10
Ashe Park (Hants) 1/57
Aske (Yorks) 1/447
Askew, G. 1/11
— I. 1/12
— Mrs M. 1/13
Askham Bryan College (Yorks). 1/377
Astbury Hall (Shrops) 1/218
Aston, S. 1/443
Astor, Mrs E. 1/16
— Hon. Gavin I. vi; 1/15
— Hon. Lt. Col. Hugh vi; ix; 1/16
— Lady I. 1/15
Attwood, Mrs A. 1/17
Auburn Hall (Lincs) 1/307
Auchenham (Ayr) 1/98
Auchterarder (Perth) 1/102
Australia 1/43; 1/252
Australian Plants Centre, Coombabah 1/448
Australian Wine Centre 1/433
Austria xii
Avens Mead (Surrey) 1/427
Aydon White House (N'land) 1/370
Aylesbury (Bucks) 1/38
Azusa (California, USA) 1/290

BBC 1/316
Bagrit, Sir Leon 1/26
Bahamas xi; 1/315; 1/458
Bahamas National Trust 1/315
Bahrain 1/149
Baillie, Maj. S. 1/27; 1/202
Bainbridge, G.V.M. 1/28
Bambouseraie de Preferance 1/442

Index of Places and People

Baker-Wilbraham, Lady 1/29
Bakewell (Derby) 1/121
Balaine, Arboretum of (France) 1/8
Baldwin, Gordon 1/222
Balfour (Angus) 1/258
Balfran, Old Manse (Stirl) 1/42; 1/379
Ballaig by Crieff (Perth) 1/266
Ballard, C.W.J. 1/381
— Helen 1/30
Balmanno (Perth) 1/68
— Castle (Perth) 1/68
Balniel, Lord Robin 1/69
Banbury (Oxon) 1/210; 1/348
Banchory (Kinc) 1/160
Bannister, D. 1/451
Banochory (Kinc) 1/74
Barber, Maj. P.N. 1/135; 1/233
Barbour, E.E. 1/202
Barclay 1/376
Barker, F.G. 1/31; 1/202
Barlaston (Staffs) 1/415
Barnard Castle (Durham) 1/385
Barnes, David 1/443
Barnham Nurseries Ltd 1/306
Barntiles (Surrey) 1/399
Barres, Arboretum des (France) 1/8; 1/457
Barry Lodge (Berks) 1/425
Basingstoke (Hants) x; xviii; 1/18; 1/57; 1/304; 1/380; 1/438
Bates, Peter 1/396
Beach, John 1/391
Beales, Peter 1/325; 1/425; 1/442
Bear Lane, London, see London
Beaulieu (Hants) 1/295
Beaulieu Palace House (Hants) 1/295
Beauly (Invern) 1/283
Beckett, Sir Martyn 1/35; 1/126; 1/138; 1/424
Beckwith Smith, Mrs 1/32
Bedale (Yorks) 1/391
— Park House 1/391
Behrens, Felicity 1/34
— Michael 1/34
— Col. W. 1/33
Biet, Lady 1/35
— Lord vi; 1/35
Beith (Ayr) 1/98
Bejing (China) 1/454
Belfast (N. Ireland) 1/378
Belgium xii; 1/81; 1/129
Belgravia, London, see London
Bell, Prof. E.A. 1/353

Bell Macdonald, Mr A.M. 1/36
Belvoir Estates Ltd 1/365
Bembridge, The Grange (Isle of Wight) 1/255
Bembridge, The Watch House (Isle of Wight) 1/170
Bemeryde (Rox) 1/175
Bentley Farm (Sussex) 1/11; 1/13
Berkhampstead (Herts) 1/172
Bernhard's Nurseries Ltd, Rugby 1/37; 1/24
Berry, Lady Pamela 1/38
Bertie, Peregrine 1/39
Beyer, R. Ian 1/450
Bhutan xviii; 1/234
Bicton Heath 1/435
Bicton Heath House (Shrops) 1/434
Biddles Ltd 1/222
Biggs, Matthew 1/450
Birdlands Zoo (Glos) 1/40
Birdsall House (N. Yorks) 1/284
Birdsey, M.R. 1/213
Birkenhead, county borough 1/189
Birley, Lady Rhoda 1/41
Bishop Wilton (Humbs) 1/188
Blackhills (Surrey) 1/399
Blackpool Tower (Lancs) 1/45
Blackrock (Co. Dublin, Eire) 1/287
Blake-Tyler, Mrs 1/44; 1/229
Blandford (Dorset) 1/159
Blechingley (Surrey) 1/245
Blessington (Co. Wicklow, Eire) 1/35
Bletchingdon (Oxon) 1/352
Bletchingdon Park (Oxon) 1/352
Bletchworth (Surrey) 1/196
Blue Hills (Bahamas) 1/315
Blyth, Betty 1/46
Bolney Lodge (Sussex) 1/426
Bolton Hall (Yorks) 1/440
Bolton's, The, No.26 1/471
Bomer, Mr 1/457
Bond, J.D. 1/224; 1/451; 1/457
Bonham-Carter, M. 1/47
Bordon (Hants) 1/428
Bostock, Mrs D. 1/48
— Mr G. 1/48
Botany Hill (Surrey) 1/286
Botches (Sussex) 1/187
Bothwell (Scotland) 1/216
Boulten and Cooper Ltd 1/100
Bourke-Borrowes, K.H. 1/56
Bourton-on-the-Water (Glos) 1/40
Bovis Construction 1/18

INDEX OF PLACES AND PEOPLE

Bowers, Mrs 1/55
Bowlby, Hon. David 1/72
— Penelope 1/72
Boyle, Capt. M.P.R. 1/57
— Lady Nell 1/57
Boynton Hall (Yorks) 1/299
Bradford Estate Forestry Dept. 1/58
Bradstock, Mrs 1/59; 1/443
Braehead 1/395
Braintree (Essex) 1/309
Braken Hill (Kent) 1/279
Bramham Park, The Little House (Yorks) 1/244
Brampton Lodge (Lincs) 1/337
Bransdale (Yorks) 1/138
Brechin (Angus) 1/258
Bredfield Place (Suff) 1/326
Brenchley, Viscountess of 1/294
Brent Cross Shopping Centre (London) 1/60
Brickell, Chris D. 1/41;1/60; 1/138; 1/199; 1/224; 1/264; 1/344
Bridge of Earn (Perth) 1/42
Bridge Walker Ltd 1/54
Bridgnorth (Shrops) 1/218; 1/239; 1/389
Bridlington (Yorks) 1/299
Bristol (Avon) 1/61
Bristol, Clifton and West of England Zoological Society 1/61
British Broadcasting Corporation, see BBC
British Transport Commission 1/249; 1/417
Broadlands 1/251
Broackes, Nigel ix; 1/49; 1/50; 1/51; 1/52; 1/53; 1/54; 1/202; 1/381; 1/359
Brockdale House (Berks) 1/39
Brocklehurst, Charles 1/63; 1/202; 1/443
Brockway, M. 1/62; 1/202
Brocton Lodge (Staffs) 1/157
Bromley-Davenport, Col. Sir W. 1/65
Brompton Hospital Sanitorium (Sussex) 1/64
Brooke, Humphrey 1/66
Brookeborough, Viscountess 1/378
Brookfield House 1/310
Brooking, Paul 1/67
Brooks, Audrey V. 1/344
Brookwood Cemetery (Surrey) 1/382
Brown, Capability ix; xvii
Brownlow, Lt Col J.D.C. 1/417
Broxbourne (Herts) 1/347
Bruce, Hon. James 1/68

Brudenell, Hon. Edmund 1/70
— Marion 1/70
Brussels, Avenue de la Renaissance (Belgium) 1/129
— Dreve des Gendarmes (Belgium) 1/81
Bryce, Mrs Ivor 1/71
Bryngwyn (Powys) 1/391
Bubwith, The Elms (Yorks) 1/320
Buchanan, John 1/18
Buckland Monachorum, The Garden House (Devon) 1/144
Bugthorpe (Yorks) 1/177
Bulman, Mr 1/443
Buntingford, The Dower House (Herts) 1/336
Burgett, James 1/73; 1/202
— Sharon 1/73
Burghclere (Hants) 1/82
Burghclere (Berks) 1/332
Burghfield Common (Berks) 1/154
Burnett of Leys, Jamie 1/74
Burnley (Lancs) 1/390
Burns, J.G. 1/207
Burnside Nursery 1/223
Burton upon Trent (Staffs) 1/7
Butler, Mrs 1/202
— Richard 1/75
— Susan 1/75
Butter, Maj. D. 1/202
— Mr David 1/76
— Myra 1/76
Bwlch-y-Cibau (Powys) 1/391

C.R. Armfield (Hull) Ltd 1/400
Cadogan Lane, London, see London
Caiger-Smith, Mr A. 1/222
Cairndow (Argyll) 1/209
Cairns, North (Queensland, Australia) 1/252
Caledonian Nurseries 1/222
Calgary House (Argyll) 1/259
Callernish House, (Outer Hebrides, Invern) 1/165
Calton Hall (Staffs) 1/7
Calvocoressi, Mrs 1/78
Cambridge, University of v
Cameron, Mr E. 1/80
— J.W. 1/443
Cameron of Lochiel, Col. D.H. 1/79
— Margaret 1/79
Campbeltown, Argyll 1/209
Campile (Co. Wexford, Eire) 1/333
Camu, Alain 1/81

INDEX OF PLACES AND PEOPLE

— Therese 1/81
Cannes (France) 1/51
Capesthorne Hall (Ches) 1/65
Cardross (Stirl) 1/318
Carlton 1/395
Carlton Husthwaite, Manor House Farm (Yorks) 1/343
Carnarvon, Earl of vi; 1/82; 1/199
Carnell (Ayr) 1/139
Carr, Mrs 1/468
Carrick Cottage (Cornw.) 1/236
Carricklee House (Co. Tyrone) 1/207
Carrigart (Co. Donegal, Eire) 1/249
Carvers (Surrey) 1/293
Castle Airy (Kinc) 1/74
Castle Cary (Guernsey) 1/432
Castle Frazer (Aberdeen) 1/464
Castle Howard (Yorks) vi; viii; ix-x; xv-xvi; xviii; 1/211; 1/214; 1/264; 1/365; 1/459
Castleacre (Norf) 1/226
Castleacre, Lord of 1/226
Caulfields Ltd 1/35; 1/417
Cayzer, Hon A. 1/443
— Bernard vi; 1/84
— Hon. M.A.R. vi; 1/83; 1/328
Cayzer House (Mddsx) 1/84
Chadshunt (Warks) 1/429
Chadwell, Chris xviii; 1/225
Chantilly (France) 1/119
Chaplain, R.M. 1/323
Chapman, A.C.B. 1/86
— Robert 1/87
— Virginia 1/87
Chapman Taylor Partners 1/53; 1/54
Chappel, P. 1/442
Chard (Soms) 1/388
Charles Funke Associates 1/149
    see also Funke, Charles
Charles L. Warren Ltd 1/189
Charleston Manor (Sussex) 1/41
Charterhouse, London see London
Charterhouse (Surrey) 1/88
Charterhouse School (Surrey) 1/398
Chase Cottage (Surrey) 1/93
Chateau de Ferrieres 1/120
Chateris, Virginia 1/89
Chatham (Kent) 1/22
Chatsworth House (Derby) 1/121
Chatto, Beth 1/90; 1/231
Chawton (Hants) 1/363
Chelsea see London
Cheltenham (Glos) 1/62

Chertsey (Surrey) 1/198
Chester (Ches) 1/182; 1/422
Chestnut Lodge (Surrey) 1/323
Cheyne Court, London, see London
Chiefswood (Rox) 1/392
Chievely Manor (Berks) 1/109
Chilstone 1/91
Chiltern Park (Victoria, Australia) 1/43
China xi; xviii, 1/151, 1/453
Chobham (Surrey) 1/110; 1/303
Cholmondeley, Marchioness of 1/92; 1/202
— Marquess of vi; 1/92
Cholmondeley Castle (Ches) xv; 1/92
Chrichton, Mrs 1/111
— Col. M. 1/111
Christies (Fachabers) Ltd 1/231
Churchill (Co. Donegal, Eire) 1/184; 1/278
Churchmead (Hants) 1/438
Clanville (Hants) 1/59
Clanville Lodge (Hants) 1/59
Cleobury Mortimer (Worcs) 1/152
Clarke, Desmond xi; 1/93
— Patsy 1/94
Claxton (Yorks) 1/420
Claxton Hall (Yorks) 1/420
Clearfast Ltd 1/328
Clifton Castle (Yorks) 1/185
Clifton Nurseries Ltd 1/95; 1/328
Clifton Vill, London, see London
Clitheroe (Lancs) 1/445
Clive, Brig. A.F.L. 1/96
Clore, Sir Charles xi; 1/97
Coates, Russell H. 1/344
Cobham (Surrey) 1/323
Cochran-Patrick, Neil 1/98
Coke, Viscount 1/99
Colchester (Essex) 1/24; 1/90
Collin, Lady Clarissa 1/100
Colombo (Sri Lanka) 1/130
Colquhalzie (Perth) 1/102
Colvin, Mrs 1/101
— M. 1/443
Comrie (Perth) 1/300; 1/349
Coneysthorpe (N Yorks) 1/312
Connell, Lady Andrew 1/102
— Lady Audrey 1/102
— J.R. 1/344
Constance Spry Ltd 1/222
Cookson, Lt. Col. J.C.V. 1/103
Coolham (Sussex) 1/107
Coombabah (Australia) 1/448

INDEX OF PLACES AND PEOPLE

Cooper, Maj. 1/104
Copex Ltd 1/400
Corbett, W. 1/105
Corbridge (N'land) 1/370
Corby (Northants) 1/70
Cornwall, Duchy of 1/106
Corsham (Wilts) 1/148
Cortachy Castle (Angus) 1/5
Corwen (Mer) 1/167
Cottage Farm (Suff) 1/183; 1/220
Cottenham, Earl of 1/107
Cotterell, Sir Richard 1/108
Country Gentlemen's Association, The 1/85
Country Life 1/427
Countryside Commission 1/130; 1/393
County Park Nursery (Essex) 1/371
Courtauld, S. 1/109
Courtney, Anthony 1/110
— Elizabeth 1/110
Cowan, Brigadier N.S. 1/223
Cowell, N. 1/18
Cowfold (Sussex) 1/83; 1/350
Cox, P. 1/202
Coxwold (Yorks) 1/437
Craignish Castle (Argyll) 1/444
Craigo by Montrose (Angus) 1/262
Craigton (Angus) 1/5
Craigwell Nurseries 1/18; 1/19; 1/24; 1/45; 1/149; 1/150
Cranborne, The Manor House (Dorset) 1/355
Crichton-Stuart, Mrs 1/112
— Maj. Michael 1/112
Cricket St Thomas (Wildlife & Leisure Park) (Soms) 1/388
Cringleford, Keswick Road (Norf) 1/86
Croom (Co. Limerick, Eire) 1/158; 1/298
Crowborough (Sussex) 1/1; 1/191
Croxden Compost Co. 1/328
Culag (Yorks) 1/275
Culham Court (Berks) 1/34
Culross (Fife) 1/131
Culross Abbey House (Fife) 1/131
Culzean Castle (Ayr) xv; 1/113
Currarevach (Surrey) 1/387
Curry Mallett (Soms) 1/201
Cutler, J.R. 1/344

d'Abo, R.E.N. 1/114
d'Unsel, Comte Philippe 1/129
Dalrymple (Ayr) 1/416
Dalswinton (Dumfr) 1/242; 1/243

Dammam Social Insurance, Saudi Arabia 1/21
Darlington (Durham) 1/441
Darwin, Robin 1/115
Daylesford House (Glos) 1/351
de Hamal, Constance 1/116
de Jong, F. 1/222
de Quincey, Mrs A. 1/117
— Capt. R.S. 1/117
de Ramsey, Lord xv; xix; 1/130; 1/229; 1/393
— Ailwyn 1/353; 1/456
de Rothschild, Madame 1/119
— E. 1/135; 1/328
— Eddie 1/344
— Edmund 1/224
— Baron Edouard 1/119
— Evelyn 1/25
— Baron Guy xvi; 1/120
— J. 1/95
— Miriam 1/224
— Victoria 1/25
Debden Manor (Essex) 1/87
Deene Park (Northants) 1/70
Deer Dell (Surrey) 1/286
Del Tedici, P. 1/263
Denchworth Manor (Berks) 1/174
Department of Transport 1/20
Derby (Derby) 1/124
Derby, Earl of 1/118
Dereham (Norf) 1/121
Diamond, H.R. 1/443
Dickhampton (Earth Moving) Ltd 1/191
Dickinson, Mr 1/244
— E. xi
Digby, Hon. Mrs Edward 1/122
Diss (Norf) 1/268
Dobbie and Co Ltd 1/381
Dodd, Tom 1/263
Donald, Duncan 1/344
Donaldson & Sons 1/60
Donegal Railways 1/249
Dorchester (Dorset) 1/122; 1/212
Dorrn, F. 1/443
Dow Flora (Singapore) Ltd 1/315; 1/449
Dowdeswells (1930) Ltd 1/222
Drew, T. 1/135
Driffield (Yorks) 1/275
Dringhouses, York 1/386
Drogheda, Earl of vi; 1/95; 1/123
Dron House (Perth) 1/68
Drummond, Mrs Maldwin 1/181

INDEX OF PLACES AND PEOPLE

Drury-Lowe, Capt. P. 1/124
Dudley, T.R. 1/263
Dudmaston (Shrops) 1/239
Duff Gordon, Sir A. 1/125
Dufferin and Ava, Marchioness of vi; 1; 126; 1/191
Dunball, A.P. 1/20
Dunbar (East Lothian) 1/173
Duncan & Davies Ltd 1/448
Duncan, Ian 1/328
Dunfermline (Fife) 1/131
Dunira, The Garden House (Perth) 1/349
Dunkeld (Perth) 1/76
Dunlewy (Co. Donegal, Eire) 1/104
Dunne, Mrs 1/128
— Henrietta 1/127
—Capt. Thomas 1/127; 1/429
—Mrs Thomas, see also Mrs Victor Willis
Dunsany Castle (Co. Meath, Eire) 1/329
Durand, Mr 1/457
Dyneley (Lancs) 1/390
E.F.G. Nurseries Ltd 1/328
E.S.G. Sales Ltd 1/272
East Clandon, The Old Parsonage (Surrey) 1/128
East Tuddenham (Norf) 1/6
Eastry (Kent) 1/271
Eastwood (Perth) 1/76
Eaton Hall (Ches) 1/422; 1/423
Edenbridge (Kent) 1/15; 1/383
Edinburgh, Royal Botanic Gardens 1/453
Edwards, Colonel 1/372
Egbury House (Hants) 1/412
Egerton, Francis 1/226
Egton Bridge (Yorks). 1/146
Egton Estates Company (Yorks). 1/146
Egton Manor (Yorks). 1/146
Eire 1/35; 1/104; 1/158; 1/184; 1/249; 1/274; 1/278; 1/296; 1/298; 1/329; 1/333; 1/417
Elgin, Lord vi
— Countess of 1/131
Eliot, Lord Peregrine 1/133
Ellens Green (Sussex) 1/73
Elmstead Market (Essex) 1/90
Elvington, The Grange (Yorks) 1/89
Elwes, Barbara 1/132
— Col. Guy 1/132
Ely Lodge (Co. Fermanagh, N. Ireland) 1/169

Elyston Court, London, see London
Emsworth and Newtown Park (Co Dublin, Eire) 1/287
Englefield Green (Surrey) 1/123
Enniskillen (Co. Fermanagh, N. Ireland) 1/111; 1/169
Enterkine House (Ayr) 1/261
Eridge Castle (Kent) 1/3
Erskine, Charlie M. 1/450
Esher (Surrey) 1/399
Eton (Berks) 1/134
Eton College (Berks) v-vi; viii; xix; 1/134
Eton Square, London, see London
Exbury Enterprises Ltd 1/135; 1/224
Exbury Gardens Ltd 1/18; 1/24; 1/135; 1/171; 1/219; 122; 1/223; 1/328; 1/452
Exbury Trees Ltd 1/442
Exotic Plants viii; xv; 1/396

F.F. Johnson and Partners 1/176
F.G. Barcock & Co. 1/332
Fabultet, Violoski 1/446
Fadmoor (Yorks) 1/138; 1/177
Faerber, Mr S. 1/136
Fairfield Lodge, Bothwell (Scotland) 1/216
Fakenham (Norf) 1/227
Falconhurst (Kent) 1/383
Falkland Palace (Fife) 1/112
Fane, M.F. 1/443
Farmington (Glos) 1/61
Farnham (Surrey) 1/286; 1/341
Fattorini, D. 1/137
Fellowes Trust 1/393
Feock (Cornw) 1/236
Ferguson, Lady, of Kilkerran 1/113
Fernil, Charles 1/315
Ferry House, The (Mddsx) 1/161
Feversham, Anne Countess of 1/138; 1/177
Fife, Maj. W.A. 1/443
Fincham (Norf) 1/457
Findlay, Mrs Eira 1/139
Finmere Construction Co. Ltd 1/126; 1/191
Firbeck, Park House (Notts) 1/321
Firma C. Esveld 1/328; 1/442
Fisher and Sons (Fakenham) Ltd 1/226
Fisher, Dowson and Wasbrough 1/71
Fisherton Delamere House (Wilts) ix; 1/44; 1/229
Fitter, Prof. Alistair vi; viii

INDEX OF PLACES AND PEOPLE

FitzAlan, Viscountess 1/140
Fitzroy, Robinson and Partners 1/150
FitzWilliam, Earl 1/141
Flat Top House (Humb) 1/187
Flaherty, E. 1/149
Fleigner, Hans J. 1/450
Fleming, Mrs A. 1/142
— Mr I. 1/142
Fletcher-Watson, J. 1/143
Flintham Hall (Notts) 1/208
Floral Mile (Singapore) 1/449
Flower House Display Ltd 1/149
Flutters Hill (Surrey) 1/198
Fochabers (Moray). 1/164
Foggo, Peter 1/224
Folly Farm (Berks) ix; 1/16
Fordel (Perth) 1/404
Forfar (Angus) 1/301
Fort Belvedere 1/246
Fortescue, L.S. 1/144
Fosbury Manor (Wilts) 1/160
Fosse Wold (Glos) 1/247
Foster, J.P. 1/130
— M. 1/381
— Michael 1/145
— Simon M. 1/146
— Mrs William 1/147
Foston, The Old Vicarage (Yorks) 1/461
Fountaine l'Abbe (France) 1/442
Fowden, Sir Leslie 1/353
Foxhill Nurseries 1/315; 1/452
France xi-xii; 1/8; 1/51; 1/119; 1/248;
    1/334; 1/442; 1/457
Francis F. Johnson & Partners 1/377;
    1/385
Fraser and Ross 1/72
Freckelton, Kirkham Road (Lancs) 1/67
Frimley (Sussex) 1/64
Friston Place (Sussex) 1/364
Fry, Drew, Knight and Creamer 1/276
Fryer, P.M. 1/19
Fujimoto, Mrs Keiko 1/224
Fuller. Lt. Col. C. 1/148
Funke, Charles 1/18; 1/19; 1/149; 1/244
    see also Charles Funke Associates
Fuse, Hideaki 1/224
Fyne Trees & Plus Trees 1/209

Gainsborough (Lincs) 1/356
— The Lawns (Lincs) 1/338
— Moreton House (Lincs)
    1/338
Galle, Fred C. 1/151; 1/315

Galliers-Pratt, Mr xvi
— Mrs 1/152
— A.M. 1/152
— G.K. 1/153
Gander & White Ltd 1/417
Gardiner, N.W. 1/154
Garns (Heref) 1/108
Garnett, Mrs A.M. 1/160
— Kit 1/160
Garrowby (Yorks). 1/176
Garrowby Hall (Yorks) 1/176
Garthmeilo (Mer) 1/167
Gaskell, R.W. 1/467
Gatacre Park (Shrops) 1/389
Gateford and Whitwell 1/321
Gateway House (Hants) 1/18
Gatley Park (Heref) 1/127
Geddes, Hon. Mrs 1/391
— F. 1/155
Gee, Hilary 1/156
Geh, S.Y. 1/130
General Accident x-xi; 1/171
Geo. Monro (Flowers) Ltd 1/222
Georgia (USA) xi
George Rainbird Ltd 1/365
George Wortley Ltd 1/457
German, Mrs Guy 1/157
Germany xi
Gibson, Michael 1/456
— Mrs J.W. 1/158
Gibson-Fleming, Maj. 1/159
— Selina 1/159
Giddy's Nursery 1/315
Gillow Manor (Heref) 1/467
Gilmour, Lady Caroline 1/161
Girling Stone Ltd 1/222
Gisborough, Lady 1/162
— Lord 1/162
Gisborough House (Clev) 1/162
Glasgow (Scotland) 1/216
Glasshouse Crops Research Institute
    1/213
Gleeds Chartered Quantity Surveyors
    1/150
Glen Phoineas (Invern) 1/283
Glenbogle Lodge (Kinc) 1/160
Glendoick Gardens Ltd 1/224; 1/328;
    1/452
Glenfarg (Perth) 1/404
Glenveagh Castle (Co Donegal, Eire)
    1/278
Glenveagh Park xii
Glook Export Services 1/442

Index of Places and People

Glyndebourne Festival Opera 1/150
Godalming (Surrey) 1/88; 1/149
Goddards, York 1/386
Godsal, Alan 1/163
— Elizabeth 1/163
Goodchild, Peter xv
Gordon Castle (Moray) 1/164
Gordon-Lennox, Mrs 1/164
Gorhambury House (Herts) 1/402
Gosford House, East Lothian 1/418
Goudhurst (Kent) 1/257
Govett, Mrs A.M. 1/160
— John 1/160
Gracious Pond (Surrey) 1/303
Grady, Cynthia 1/449
Granville, Earl 1/165
Great Auclam (Berks) 1/154
Great Burton Hall (Lincs) 1/356
Great Easton Manor (Leics) 1/237
Great Linford Manor (Berks) 1/91
Great Missenden (Bucks) 1/155
Great Westwood (Herts) 1/83
Green Farm (Norf) 1/6
Green, Peter S. 1/453
Green, Mrs Robert 1/166
Greenfields 1/345
Grenfell, D. 1/194
Grey's Cottage (Oxon) 1/190
Griffiths, Mrs D.H. 1/167
Grimsby (Lincs) 1/72
Grose, Mrs 1/168
Grosvenor, Col. R.G. 1/169
— Viola 1/169
Guernsey 1/432
Guisborough (Yorks) 1/162
Guisborough Hall (Yorks) 1/162
Gunston, Lady 1/170
Gutteridge, G.E. 1/117

H. Pannet (Eastbourne) Ltd 1/191
H.C. Aubrey & Sons 1/34
H.J. Hatfield & Sons Ltd 1/213
H.W. Dean and Son 1/332
Haarlem (The Netherlands) 1/400
Haddington, Countess of, Sarah 1/173
— Lord vi
Haddon Hall 1/365
Haddon-Paton, Maj. A.G.N. 1172
Hague, Maj. Derek 1174
Haig, Countess 1/175
Haines Hill (Berks) 1/163
Halifax, Earl of 1/176
— Dowager Countess of 1/177

Halkin St, London, *see* London
Hall, Mary 1/452
— P. 1/178
Halland (Sussex) 1/11; 1/13
Halliwell, Brian 1/450
Halls Home and Gardens 1/385
Halstead (Essex) 1/75
Halstead, A.J. 1/344
Ham Spray House (Wilts) 1/132
Hamal, de *see* de Hamal
Hambleden, Lady 1/179
— Viscount vi; 1/180
Hambleden, The Manor House (Oxon) 1/179; 1/180
Hamill, W.H. 1/378
Hamilton, Georgia and Callaway Gardens, (Georgia, USA) 1/151
Hammill Farm (Kent) 1/271
Hampshire Gardens Trust 1/181
Hampstead, London, *see* London
Hanbury Williams, Mrs 1/381
— Mrs D. 1/182
— Mrs J.A. 1/182
Hare, Hon. John 1/183; 1/220
Hare Hill (Ches) xix; 1/63
Harewood End (Heref) 1/467
Harker-Taylor Services 1/384
Harleyburn (Rox) 1/27
Harlow Car (Yorks) 1/452
Harmsworth, Hon. Vere 1/200
Harpenden (Herts) 1/353
Harpton Court (Radn) 1/125
Harris, Doug 1/82; 1/135
— J. Gordon S. 1/201
— K.M. 1/344
Harrogate (Yorks) 1/305; 1/330; 1/339
Hascombe (Surrey) 1/271
Haskard, O. 1/138; 1/202
Haslemere (Surrey) 1/93; 1/293; 1/387
Hastings, Lord vi; 1/203
Havant (Hants) 1/19
Haven House (Kent) 1/235
Havenfield (Bucks) 1/155
Haverhill (Suff) 1/71
Hawick (Rox) 1/46
Haywards Heath (Sussex) 1/215
Healing, The Manor (Lincs) 1/72
Heathcoat-Armory, Brig. R. 1/204
Heckfield (Hants) 1/380
Hedley, Gill 1/181
Helmsley (Yorks) 1/138
Henderson, J.P.R 1/205
— N. 1/202

INDEX OF PLACES AND PEOPLE

— Sarah 1/205
— Sir William 1/352
Henley on Thames (Oxon) 1/179; 1/180; 1/192
Hennell, Percy 1/365
Herbert, Hon G. 1/332
Herdman, Dorothy 1/207
Hereford 1/108
Hergest Croft Gardens 1/328
Heron's Ghill (Sussex) 1/200
Heseltine, Rt. Hon. Michael 1/210
Hever Castle (Kent) 1/15
Hexham (N'land) 1/94
Higgins, David 1/203; 1/415
— T.D. 1/443
Highclere Castle (Berks) xii; 1/82
Highfield Park (Hants) 1/380
Highgrove (Glos) 1/106
Highworth (Wilts) 1/31
Hildyard, Myles T. 1/208
Hill, A. Robin I. 1/185
— Derek 1/184
Hillier Arboretum (Hants) xii; xix; 1/181; 1/199; 1/457
Hillier Nurseries 1/224
Hilliers & Sons (Winchester) Ltd 1/231; 1/306; 1/332
Hindlip, Viscount vi
— Viscountess 1/187
Hobbs and Chambers 1/142
Hogg Robinson (UK) Ltd 1/214; 1/315
Holderness, Lord Richard 1/188
Holford House (Sussex) 1/317
Holkham Hall (Norf) 1/99
Holland, see Netherlands, The
Holland-Hibbert, Mrs I. 1/186
— Hon. J. 1/186
Holliday, Mrs L.B. 1/206
Holmwood (Worcs) 1/342
Holt, G.P. 1/189
Holt Memorial Garden (Lancs) xvii; 1/189
Holy Hill (Co Tyrone, N Ireland) 1/4
Holywood (Dumf) 1/231
Honan, Mrs 1/95
Honey Brothers Ltd 1/315
Hope, Lady John 1/190
Hopewell-Ash, T. 1/222; 1/223
Hopkin, Harold C. 1/263
Horder Arthritic Centre (Sussex) 1/191
Horlick, Col. Sir James 1/192
Hornchurch (Essex) 1/371
Horsham (Sussex) 1/101

Horsman, John 1/171; 1/209; 1/269
Horstead Place (Sussex) 1/308
Horton, Mrs 1/193
Hosta & Hemerocallis Society (British) 1/194
Hotchkin, N.S. 1/195
Houghton Hall (Yorks). 1/140; 1/270
Houndsell Place (Sussex) 1/1
House and Garden 1/222
House of Glennie, The (Aberdeen) 1/302
Hovingham (Yorks) 1/439
Hovingham Hall (Yorks) 1/439
Howard, George v; viii; ix; 1/328
— Simon 1/264
Howard de Walden, Lady 1/196
Howell, J. Bede 1/197
Hubble, Helen 1/396
Hull Foot (Lancs) 1/445
Hungerhill House (Sussex) 1/107
Hunters Solicitors 1/308
Huntly (Aberdeen) 1/302
Hurlford by Kilmarnock (Ayr) 1/139
Hurst, Margery 1/198
Hush Heath Manor (Kent) 1/257
Hutchinson, Brian 1/328
Huttons Ambo, The Grange (Yorks) 1/219
Huxley (Ches) 1/182
Huxley Lane Farm (Ches) 1/182
Hyde, N.H. 1/393
Hyde Park Gate, London, see London
Hydon Nurseries Ltd 1/171; 1/452

IBM 1/19; 1/23
I.C.I. 1/443
I.W. Cole and Son 1/222
Ida Casson Callaway Foundation, USA 1/151
Ideal Homes Exhibition xii; xviii; xix; 1/222; 1/223
Ilchester, Countess of 1/212
Ilchester Place, London, see London
Illet, K.G. 1/18; 1/19; 1/24
Imperial Chemical Industries, see I.C.I.
Impetus Garden Furniture Ltd 1/222
Inholmes (Yorks) 1/346
Inish Rath, N. Ireland 1/360
International Dendrology Society xi; 1/279
International Versepuy (France) 1/403
Internationales Burgen-Institut Historical Gardens Exhibition 1/211
Ipswich (Suff) 1/183; 1/220

INDEX OF PLACES AND PEOPLE

Inverinate (Scotland) 1/72
Irving, M.K. 1/443
Islanmore (Co Limerick, Eire) 1/298
Isle of Gigha (Argyll) xix; 1/192; 1/242
Isle of Jura 1/346
Isle of Mull 1/215; 1/259
Isle of Wight 1/170
Isleworth (Mddsx) 1/161; 1/313
Ives, Patricia 1/450
Ivy Lodge (Warks) 1/429

J. Scott & Co. 1/339
Jaggards (Wilts) 1/148
James A. Crabtree & Associates 1/191
James Laurie & Sons 1/171
James Parr & Partners 1/171
James, Hon. David 1/215
— Jacquetta 1/215
— Jeremy 1/443
— Jocelyn 1/451
Japan ix-x; xii; 1/224; 1/451
Jarvie, R.W.G. 1/216
Jekyll, Gertrude ix; xvii; 1/325
Jellicoe, Countess 1/202
— Earl George 1/217
— Countess Philippa 1/217
Jenks, D. Brian 1/218
Jenyns, Kathleen 1/219
Jermyns House Appeal 1/181; 1/199
Jodrell Bank (Ches) 1/254
— Arboretum (Ches) xi; 1/254
John Black Ltd 1/329
John German & Son 1/417; 1/431
John Huggan & Co. Lt. 1/342
John Waterer Sons & Crisp Ltd vii; 1/42; 1/54; 1/231; 1/367; 1/438; 1/443
Johns Inc. 1/332
Jones, Mr 1/16
— J.E. 1/252
— Paul 1/54
— W.G. 1/222
Jong, de *see* de Jong
Joseph Bentley Ltd 1/136
Josiah Wedgwood & Sons Ltd, Stoke on Trent (Staffs) 1/415
see also Wedgewood, Hon. Josiah
Juniper Hill (Bucks) 1/322

Kalorama (Victoria, Australia) 1/43
Kashmir xviii; 1/225
Keele, University of (Staffs) 1/156
Keely, Mr 1/443

Keir and Cawdor Ltd 1/202
Keith Starr Alpines 1/371
Keith, Caroline 1/227
— David A. 1/227; 1/443
— Kenneth 1/226
Kendell Stone and Paving Co Ltd 1/222
Kennedy, Mrs 1/238
—Mrs M. 1/360
Kensington Palace Gardens, London, *see* London
Kent House (Norf) 1/86
Kent, H.R.H the Duchess of 1/228
Ker, David 1/229
Kern, Joseph 1/230
Kessing, J.L.S. 1/450
Keswick, Clare 1/231
— David 1/231
— J. 1/202
— John 1/222; 1/223; 1/231
— Maggie 1/232
Kew, London 1/450
 see also Royal Botanic Gardens
Khaled, King 1/233
Kidderminster (Worcs). 1/152
Kildangon (Co Kildare, Eire) 1/296
Killyreagh (Co Fermanagh, N Ireland) 1/111
Kilmarnock (Ayr) 1/238
Kilmokea House (Co Wexford, Eire) 1/333
Kimball, Marcus 1/237
Kineton (Warks) 1/429
King, E. 1/443
Kingoldrum (Forf) 1/462
King's Bench Walk, London, *see* London
King's Langley (Herts) 1/83
King's Lynn (Norf) 1/147; 1/226; 1/228; 1/273; 1/457
Kinmouth, Fergus xviii; 1/234
Kinnersley, Charles 1/236
Kintbury (Berks) 1/425
Kippen (Stirl) 1/315
Kirkwood, Sir Robert 1/235
Kirriemuir (Angus) 1/5
Kitchingham, R.M. 1/194
Knaphill Nursery Ltd 1/332
Knight, Lynn 1/450
Knowsley Hall (Lancs) 1/118
Kurashige, Yuji 1/224
Kyles of Lochalsh (Scotland) 1/72

La Bastide de la Roquette (France) 1/51
La Playa (Bahamas) 1/315

INDEX OF PLACES AND PEOPLE

Labouchere, Lady 1/223
— Lady Rachel 1/239
Laguna (Perth) 1/369
Lamberhurst (Kent) 1/126
Lambert, Mrs 1/134
— Capt. P 1/443
— Uvedale 1/245
Lambton, Lady Elizabeth 1/240
Lancaster, Anne 1/241
— Mrs O. 1/443
— Osbert 1/241
— Roy 1/451
Land of Nod, The (Hants) 1/428
Lane Fox, Mrs 1/244
Lanfine (Ayr) 1/352
Langlois, Mrs 1/315
Lansdale, Beatrice 1/243
— David 1/242
Lapoinya (Tasmania) 1/265
Lascelles, Hon. Mrs G. 1/246
Lauder (Berwick) 1/27
Lavers Hill (Australia) 1/414
Lazenby, Rosemary 1/247
le Rougetel 1/454
Lebreton, Michael 1/442
Lecoufle, Marcel 1/248; 1/342
  see also Marcel Lecoufle Orchidees
Leighton Buzzard (Beds). 1/25
Leinthall Earls (Heref) 1/127
Leitrim, Anne Countess of 1/249
Leominster (Heref) 1/127
Les Floriales (Monte Carlo) 1/97
Lesbury House (N'land) 1/324
Leslie, A.C. 1/344
Letchworth, Icknield Way West, Herts 1/85
Letterkenny (Co Donegal, Eire) 1/278
Leveson, Mrs A. 1/351
Leveson-Gower, Mrs R. 1/250
Lewes (Sussex) 1/11; 1/12; 1/13; 1/277
Lewis, Alan W. 1/323
Lexham Hall (Norf) 1/147
Leysthorpe (Yorks). 1/145
Lichfield Downs (Hants) 1/430
Lietrim, Countess of 1/443
Limberlost Nurseries 1/252; 1/315
Linaskea (N. Ireland) 1/360
Lincoln 1/307; 1/405
Lindsay, Hon. Lady Loelia 1/253
Linsey (Lincs) 1/195
Lion Brewery, Hartlepool 1/443
Lion Place (Mddsx) 1/161
Little Aston (Warks) 1/136

Little Barrow (Glos) 1/266
Little Blakenham (Suff) 1/183; 1/220
Little Dunbarnie (Perth) 1/42
Liverpool (Lancs) 1/189
Llanfyllin (Powys) 1/391
Llangwyn (Mer) 1/167
Llanrwst (N. Wales) 1/2
Lloyds 1/22
Lloyds Bank Ltd x; 1/150; 1/339
Lochearnhead (Perth) 1/3/4
Lockerbie (Dumf) 1/36
Lockinge (Berks) 1/256
Locko Park, Derbys 1/124
Lombard North Central Ltd 1/214
London 1/60
— Airport 1/329
— Bear Lane 1/366
— Belgravia 1/138
— Cadogan Lane 1/332
— Charterhouse 1/88
— Chelsea 1/232
— Chelsea Square 1/52
— Cheyne Court 1/241
— Clifton Vill 1/95
— Elyston Court 1/168
— Eton Square 1/241
— Halkin Street 1/335
— Hampstead 1/69
— Hyde Park Gate xv; 1/50
— Ilchester Place 1/83; 1/280
— Kensington Palace Gardens 1/289
— King's Bench Walk 1/294
— Pelham Crescent 1/66
— Phillimore Gardens 1/354
— Royal Crescent Mews 1/234
— Royal Hospital Road 1/241
— St Mary Axe 1/84
— South End 1/455
— Temple 1/294
— Victoria Road 1/47
— Wilton Row 1/161
Long Ashton 1/450
Long Cross (Surrey) 1/198
Long Ford Hall (Shrops) 1/178
Long Parish (Hants) 1/373
Longniddry (East Lothian) 1/418
Longnor Hall (Shrops) 1/9
Longnor, Dower House (Derbys) 1/105
Lonsdale, Mr 1/453
Loughbrow House (N'land) 1/94
Louis Grey & Match 1/77
Loundon Road 1/401
Lovell, Sir Bernard 1/254

INDEX OF PLACES AND PEOPLE

Lowesby Hall (Leics) 1/315
Lowry-Corry, Maj. Monty 1/255
Loyd, C.L. 1/256
— Julian 1/357
Lucas, Otto 1/257
Lumsden, G.R.C. 1/258
Lushill House (Wilts) 1/31
Luton (Beds) 1/419
Luton Hoo (Beds) 1/419
Luwsa (Hydroculture) Ltd 1/342
Luzarches (France) 1/334
Lydrey (Glos) 1/384
Lyford Clay (Bahamas) 1/315

M.A.T. Transport 1/223
M.J. Aller and Sons Ltd 1/272
Macclesfield (Ches) 1/61; 1/65; 1/254
Macbeath, J. 1/466
McCarthy, John 1/181
McClintock, David 1/279
McCorquadale, Mrs 1/280
McDaniel, J.C. 1/263
MacDonald, Hon. Mrs M. 1/260
McGrath, Mrs 1/281
McGuire, J.D. 1/287
McIlhenny, Henry P. 1/202; 1/278
MacKenzie, Cathie E. 1/202
— Elizabeth 1/259
— Eric 1/259
McLafferty, Mrs 1/278
MacPherson-Grant, Sir Euan 1/262
McQuire, John F. 1/286
Mackie, Hon. Mrs Alan 1/261
Madagascar xi
Maenan Hall (North Wales) 1/2
Magnolia Society (America) 1/263
Mairs, Col. A. 1/43
Major, John 1/264
Mallet Court Nursery (Soms) 1/201
Malmaison Wine Club 1/433
Malone, Bob 1/265
Malpas (Ches) 1/92
Malton (N Yorks) 1/33; 1/284; 1/377
Malton Festival Office 1/315
Malvern (Worcs) 1/30
Manchester (Lancs) 1/361
— University of 1/254
Mancroft, Diana 1/442
Mander, Sir Charles 1/266
Mann, Lady Clare 1/267
— George 1/267
— Margaret 1/267
Manoir Sans Souci (France) 1/119

Mansfield, Earl of 1/269
Manson, Maurice 1/457
Manton, Lady Mary 1/270
Marcel Lecoufle Orchidees 1/248
Marcus House (Angus) 1/301
Marden (Heref) 1/117
Marecco, Ann 1/274
— Anthony 1/274
Mark Cross (Sussex) 1/1
Market Harborough (Leics) 1/237
Marks & Spencer Ltd ix; 1/328
Marks, Ann 1/270
Marks, J.F.E. 1/272; 1/393; 1/456
Markwell, C.R. 1/273
— P.P. 1/457
— P. 1/273
Marlborough (Wilts) 1/132; 1/160; 1/217; 1/431
Marriott, Richard 1/299
Marshall Sisson 1/130; 1/272
Marston, David 1/275
— Joan K. 1/275
Martinique xi
Maryland 1/460
Maryville (Co Limerick, Eire) 1/158
Mason, M. 1/199
Mathon (Wales) 1/30
Mattock, John 1/41
Maude, John 1/126
Mauritius xviii; 1/276
Mawley Hall (Worcs) 1/152; 1/154
May, Betty 1/277
— Hugh 1/277
Maybole (Ayr) 1/113
Mayers, D.E. 1/452
Megginson. J.R. 1/393
Melbury House (Dorset) 1/212
Meldon Park (N'land) 1/103
Melgund Glen (Rox) 1/46
Melrose (Rox) 1/27; 1/175; 1/392
Melton Mowbray (Leics) 1/311
Menmuir (Angus) 1/258
Mentor (Ohio, USA) 1/230
Merry, Mrs Eion 1/283
Merton, John 1/282
— Penelope 1/282
Messenger & Co Ltd 1/192; 1/278
Mestrallet, Henri 1/442
Mexico xi; 1/457
Meyer, Dr Fred G. 1/189; 1/332
Middleton, C. 1/451
— Lady Janet 1/284
— M. 1/451

INDEX OF PLACES AND PEOPLE

— Lord Michael 1/284
— P.S. 1/181
Middlesex Hospital 1/285
Miki Travel Agency 1/224
Milford Lake House (Berks) 1/82; 1/332
Mill Lane Nursery 1/442
Millais, E.G. 1/224
Miller-Mundy, Maj. Peter 1/202; 1/288
Mills, Mrs G.B. 1/289
Milton Hall (Northants) 1/141
Ming Park Close Estate 1/452
Ministry of Agriculture 1/291; 1/292; 1/315
Ministry of Agriculture, N Ireland 1/378
Ministry of Finance, N Ireland 1/378
Minterne (Dorset) 1/122
Minto (Rox) 1/46
Mitchell, Alan 1/264
Mocatta, Pamela 1/293
Monasterevan (Co Kildare, Eire) 1/296
Monckton, Bridget, Viscountess of Brenchley 1/294
Monro Horticultural Sundries Ltd 1/165
Monrovia Nurseries Co, USA 1/290
Montague, Lord 1/295
Monte Carlo xi; 1/97
Montrose, M. 1/213
More O'Ferrall, Roderic 1/296
Moreton in the Marsh (Glos) 1/266; 1/351
Moreton Morrel (Warks) 1/193
Morley, Derek 1/297; 1/298
— Marie-Josee 1/297; 1/298
Morpeth (N'land) 1/103; 1/314
Mortimer (Berks) 1/240
Mortimer Hill (Berks) 1/240
Mortimer House 1/49; 1/366
Mostyn-Owen, W. 1/300
Moulton-Barrett, Mrs 1/302
Mount Agaki Nature Observation Park (Japan) x; 1/224
Mount Armstrong 1/94
Mount Ledge 1/77
Mount St John (Yorks). 1/206
Mountgarrett, Viscountess 1/305
Mowbray & Stourton, Lady 1/202
— Lord Charles 1/301
— Lady Jane 1/301
Moyns Park (Suff) 1/71
Muir Smith, Mrs E. 1/303
Mulholland, Hon. Mrs John 1/304
Mulroy (Co Donegal, Eire) 1/249
Munden (Herts) 1/186

Murrells of Shrewsbury 1/305; 1/437
Murthley (Perth) 1/369

Nafferton, Green Lane (Yorks) 1/275
Naito, Tsunekata 1/224
Nakamura, Tsuneo 1/224
Nantclwyd (Denb) 1/306
Nantclwyd Hall (Denb) 1/306
Nassau (Bahamas) xi; 1/315; 1/458
National Council for the Conservation of Plants and Gardens 1/384
National Trust 1/25; 1/172; 1/323
National Trust for Scotland xv; 1/113; 1/138; 1/365
Nawton Towers (Yorks) 1/138
Naylor Leyland, Sir Vivyan 1/306
Neadley (Hants) 1/428
Neasham Hall (Durham) 1/441
Neo Plants Ltd 1/67
Nether Underwood (Ayr) 1/238
Netherlands, The xii; 1/13; 1/400
Nevile, H.N. 1/307
— Lady Rupert vii; 1/308
New Place (Glos) 1/61
New Plymouth (New Zealand) 1/448
New Zealand 1/448
Newark (Notts) 1/208
Newburgh Priory (Yorks). 1/437
Newbury, Richard 1/385
Newbury (Berks) 1/32; 1/109; 1/205; 1/267; 1/332; 1/425
Newbury (Hants) 1/82
Newby Hall Estate 1/365
Newman, Comm. 1/309
— Lady Joan 1/309
Newmilns (Ayr) 1/352
Newport (Shrops) 1/178
Newport Pagnell (Bucks) 1/91
Newton Grange (Staffs) 1/116
Newton Regis (Staffs) 1/116
Nicholls, Mrs 1/310
Nicholson, Nigel 1/359
Nippress Forwarding Ltd 1/328
Noel, G.L.G. 1/323
Norman, Mrs 1/312
— Capt. E.D. 1/312
— Hon. Mrs Willoughby 1/311
Normandy (France) ix; xi; 1/442
North Chailey (Sussex) 1/317
North Harbour (Hants) 1/23
North Scotland College of Agriculture, The 1/165

INDEX OF PLACES AND PEOPLE

North Uist, Outer Hebrides (Invern) 1/165
Northcutts Nurseries xv
Northern Police Convalescent Home 1/330
Northumberland, Duke of xvi; 1/313
— Duchess of xvi; 1/313
Northwich (Ches) 1/10
Norton, Vera 1/314
Norwich (Norf) 1/86
Notcutts Nurseries Ltd 1/224
Nuffield (Oxon) 1/192
Nuffield Radio Astronomy Laboratories 1/254
Nuttall, Sir Nicholas xi; 1/315

O.A.D. Agriculture Ltd 1/45; 1/358
O'Keeffe, Paddy 1/316
Oakland, La Salle Ave (California, USA) 1/166
Oare (Wilts) 1/282
Oare House (Wilts) 1/282
Ocean Management Services Ltd 1/189
Ocean Steam Ship Company 1/189
Okada, Peter K. 1/224
Old Country (Worcs) 1/30
Old Isleworth (Mddsx) 1/115
Old Windsor, The Dower House (Dorset) 1/394
Onslow Hall (Shrops) 1/435
Ormiston, Alan 1/317
— Ursula 1/317
Orr-Ewing, Lady 1/318
— Maj. Sir Ronald 1/318
Osbaldwick (Yorks) 1/145
Osbaldwick Hall (Yorks) 1/204
Osbourne and Co. 1/278
Otway Ridge Arboretum (Australia) 1/414
Outer Hebrides 1/165
Oving House (Berks) 1/38
Owl House, The (Kent) 1/126
Oxford, St Aldates 1/392
Oxted (Surrey) 1/427

P. Chappell 1/328
Padt, J. 1/344
Palm Centre, The 1/315
Panfield Hall (Essex) 1/309
Paris, France 1/248
Parkinson, Marjorie 1/319
— Stuart 1/320
Parkside House (Surrey) 1/123

Paton, Mr 1/5
Paul Temple Ltd 1/223
Paul, G.H. 1/443
Peacock Hills (Sussex) 1/101
Pearson and Ward 1/19
Peech, Neil M. 1/321
— Peggy 1/321
Pelham Crescent, London, see London
Pelly, E. 1/322
Pembroke House (Surrey) 1/110
Penn (Bucks) 1/322
Pennington, C.H. 1/381
Penny Pot (Essex) 1/75
Pennyholme (Yorks) 1/138; 1/177
Penwood Nurseries 1/82
Percy, Sir Richard 1/324
— Lady Richard xvi
— Lady Sarah 1/324
Perkins, Mrs 1/325
Perry Lionel 1/417
Perrystone Court (Heref) 1/96
Pershore, Broad Street (Worcs) 1/197
Peterborough 1/141
Pfaffman, G.A 1/263
Philimore, Hon. Claude 1/118; 1/203
Phillimore Gardens, London see London
Philip Jebb 1/315
Pickwell Manor (Leics) 1/311
Pilditch, Dennis 1/326
— Joyce 1/326
Pilgrims Way (Surrey) 1/341
Pillowell (Glos) 1/384
Pine Mountain (Georgia, USA) 1/151
Pinto, Mrs Gladys 1/327
Pirrie, Lindsey 1/18
Pitheablis (Perth) x; 1/171
Platt (Kent) 1/279
Plumpton Place 1/325
Plunkett, Col. Randall vii; 1/329
Pockley (Yorks) 1/100
Pole, Richard Carew 1/133
Pollitzer, G.E. 1/331
Polytechnic of the South Bank 1/18
Ponsonby, Laura 1/450; 1/455; 1/456
Pope, Mrs 1/465
Porchester, Lord 1/332
Port Eliot (Cornw.) 1/133
Port Hall, Co Donegal, Eire 1/274
Port of Menteith Station (Stirl) 1/318
Portrack House, Dumfr. 1/231
Portsmouth (Hants) 1/23
— H M Naval Base (Hants) 1/20
Powell, A.P.C. 1/225

INDEX OF PLACES AND PEOPLE

Powton, Eileen 1/264
Prescot (Lancs) 1/118
Presteigne (Radn) 1/125
Preston (Lancs) 1/451
Price, D.E.C. 1/333
Prideaux, Julian 1/25
— John 1/25
Priest, Jim 1/334
  Sylvia 1/334
Priestman, Mrs 1/335
Proby, P. 1/134
Profumo, Jack 1/202; 1/336; 1/381
— Valerie 1/336
Pumfrey, Mrs. J.A. 1/337
— Marie-Therese 1/338
— Paul 1/338
Pycraft, G. 1/344

Qing, Mr Ching 1/454
Quaives, The (Kent) 1/297
Quaymont Ltd 1/273; 1/457
Quincy, de see de Quincy
Quinta, The (Ches) 1/254

R. Panichelli and Sons 1/222
R.H.S. (Royal Horticultural Society) xii; 1/344; 1/359
— Enterprises 1/224
— Wisley 1/365
see also Wisley
R.V. Roger Ltd 1/162; 1/176
Radcliffe, Capt. J.B.E. 1/339
Radford, Rob 1/265
Radway (Warks) 1/429
Rainbird, George xi; 1/340
Rammerscales (Dumf) 1/36
Ramsbury Manor (Wilts) 1/431
Ramsey (Hunt) 1/272
Ramsey, de see de Ramsey
Ranston (Dorset) 1/159
Rathdonnell (Co Donegal, Eire) 1/417
Raversley, Mrs 1/202
Rawlence and Squarey 1/203
Ray Wood xviii
Read, Brig. E. 1/341
Read's Nursery 1/315
Reading (Berks) 1/34
Red Lion Bookshop 1/224
Redditch, Plymouth Road (Worcs) 1/342
Redditch Development Corporation x; xvii; 1/342
Reid, Mrs 1/343
— Lt. Col. J.W. 1/343

Richardson, Col. F. 1/345
Richmond (Yorks) 1/447
Riley-Smith, Mrs T.A. 1/346
Ripon (Yorks) 1/185; 1/250
Riyadh (Saudi Arabia) 1/470
Robert Green Gerard Ltd 1/222
Roberts, G.P. Hardy 1/285
Robinson, Mr 1/457
— S.F.T.L. 1/202
Rochford, see Thomas Rochford & Sons Ltd
Rocksavage xv
Rode Hall (Ches) 1/29
Roecliff Lodge 1/28
Rootes, T.D. 1/348
Roper, Lanning xii; 1/278
Ropner, Lady Auriol 1/391
Rose, Lt. Col. A.J.C. 1/349
— Mrs M. 1/349
Ross (Heref) 1/96
Rossway (Herts) 1/172
Rothamsted Experimental Station 1/353
Rotherfield Grey's (Oxon) 1/190
Rotherham (Yorks) 1/359
Rothermere, Viscount xii; xix; 1/351
Rotherwick, Dowager Lady 1/350
— Lord vi; 1/352
Rothschild, see de Rothschild
Rothwell, R.F. 1/443
Royal College of Art, London 1/115
Royal Crescent Mews, London, see London
Royal Hospital Rd, London, see London
Royal Horticultural Society, see R.H.S.
Royal Horticultural Society of Japan x
Royal Botanic Gardens 1/453
— Kew 1/450; 1/457
— Wakehurst Place 1/453
Royal Moerheim Nurseries 1/278
Royaumont, Les Ecuries, France 1/334
Ruckley Grange (Shrops) 1/17
Rudding Park (Yorks) 1/339; 1/365
Rudgwick (Sussex) 1/73
Rugby (Warks) 1/37
Russborough (Co Wicklow, Eire) 1/35
Russborough House (Co Donegal, Eire) 1/104
Russell James Philip Cuming v-xx
Ryders Wells Farm (Sussex) 1/277
Ryedale Travel 1/315
Ryhead 1/233
Rystwood House 1/331
Rzedowski, J. 1/263

INDEX OF PLACES AND PEOPLE

Sacher, Mrs Michael 1/354
Saffron Walden (Essex) 1/87
Saighton Grange (Ches) 1/422
St Albans (Herts) 1/402
St Boswells (Rox) 1/175
St Columb (Co Donegal, Eire) 1/184
St Germans (Cornw.) 1/133
St Germans, Earl of 1/133
St Lucia xii
St Mary Axe, London, *see* London
St Mary Bourne (Hants) 1/412
Sales, D.J. 1/264
— John 1/25
Salisbury, Marchioness of 1/355
Samlesbury 1/451
Sancton (Yorks) 1/140; 1/270
Sandars, J.E. 1/356
— M. 1/356
Sandbeck Park (Yorks) 1/359
Sander, John 1/222
Sanders, Mrs 1/202
— John 1/344
Sanderson, R.F. 1/202
Sandringham (Norf) 1/357
Sandwich (Kent) 1/235; 1/271
Sato, Hiroyuki 1/224
Saudi Arabia 1/21; 1/358; 1/470
Saville, Sir E. 1/135
Savill, Sir Eric 1/222
Sawley Hall (Yorks) 1/137
Scarbrough, Earl of 1/359
Scheunert, Col. Kot vii; 1/360
— Ruth 1/360
Schilling, Anthony D. 1/450; 1/453
Scholar Green (Ches) 1/29
Schollick, Very Revd Canon 1/361
Scone Palace (Perth) 1/269
Scott 1/362
Seaford (Sussex) 1/38
Seaton Delaval Hall (N'land) vi; 1/203
Seibu Akagi Botanical Institute 1/224
Seiyo Corporation, Japan x; 1/135; 1/224
Selby (Yorks) 1/320
Send, The Old Vicarage (Surrey) xix; 1/253; 1/424
Seneviratne, Dr V. 1/130
Serquigny (France) 1/442
Settrington House (Yorks) 1/377
Sevenhampton (Wilts) 1/142
Sevenhampton Place (Wilts) 1/142
Sevenoaks (Kent) 1/279
Sezincote (Glos) 1/473

Shan, Fan Jiu 1/450
Sharples, Mrs 1/363
Sharpthorne (Sussex) 1/15
Shawcross, Lady 1/364
Shawell House (N'land) 1/370
Sheffield, I.M.C. 1/451
Shell Gardens 1/365
Sheringham Hall (Norf) 1/397
Sherriff, Mrs 1/462
Shifnal (Shrops) 1/17; 1/58
Shipston-on-Stour (Warks) 1/340
Shrewsbury (Shrops) 1/9; 1/305; 1/434; 1/435
Siddeley Landscapes 1/366
Siddeley, Rt Hon. Randle 1/366
Simmons, John B. 1/450; 1/453
Singapore 1/130; 1/449
Singapore Botanic Gardens 1/130
Sissinghurst Castle (Kent) 1/56; 1/365
Sitwell, Francis 1/367
— Georgia 1/367
— Sir Sacheverell vi; 1/202; 1/367
Skeldon House (Ayr) 1/416
Slaley (N'land) 1/335
Slaley Hall (N'land) 1/335
Sleningford Grange (Yorks) 1/250
Slieve Donard Nurseries and Co. Ltd 1/207; 1/378
Smallcombe, P.G.E. 1/457
Smiley 1/463
Smith and Norwood 1/362
Smith, Mrs 1/369
— George W. 1/386
— Ian 1/368
— V. Russell 1/54; 1/165; 1/189; 1/213; 1/235; 1/438
Smithers, P. 1/202; 1/263
Smiths-Gore 1/244; 1/377; 1/385
Sollas, Outer Hebrides (Invern) 1/165
Sonning, The Deanery (Berks) ix; 1/53
South Africa 1/449
South End, London, *see* London
South Godstone (Surrey) 1/375
South Park (Surrey) 1/245
South Park Farm (Surrey) 1/375
South Staineley (Yorks) 1/305
Southern Graves 1/332
Southfield Farm (Hants) 1/363
Sparsholt Manor (Berks) 1/288
Spear Bridge (Invern) 1/79
Speight, Mr 1/463
Speke, Mrs 1/370
— Col. N.H.R. 1/370

INDEX OF PLACES AND PEOPLE

Sri Lanka xi; 1/130
Stafford (Staffs) 1/157
Staineley House (Yorks) 1/305
Staines (Mddsx) 1/149
Stamford Bridge (Yorks) 1/436
Stanley and Co. 1/72
Stapeley Water Gardens Ltd 1/19
Starr, Keith 1/371
   see also Keith Starr Alpines
Stathern and Blair 1/372
Station Parade 1/77
Steeple Bumpstead (Suff) 1/71
Steetley Company Ltd 1/321
Stevens, Jocelyn 1/372
Stevenson, Rosa 1/372
Stewards (Ferndawn) Nurseries Ltd 1/394
Stewart, Mrs 1/376
— Maj. John 1/374
Stewart-Smith, Pamela 1/375
— Tom 1/325
Stockwell, L.A. 1/18; 1/24; 1/135
Stoke on Trent (Staffs) 1/415
Stones Place, Lincoln 1/405
Storey, Sir Richard 1/328; 1/377
— Virginia 1/377
Stormont House, Belfast 1/378
Stott and Ward Ltd 1/189
Strabane (Co. Tyrone, N Ireland) 1/4
Stratford-upon-Avon (Warks) 1/421
Streatley-on-Thames (Berks) 1/241
Stronguet Point (Cornw.) 1/236
Stow on the Wold (Glos) 1/247
Stroods (Sussex) 1/200
Stuart Low and Co Ltd 1/222
Stuart-Black, Maj. A.A. 1/380
— Maj. I.Hervey 1/42; 1/379
Sulhamstead (Berks) 1/16
Sullinstead, The Old Rectory (Berks) 1/32
Sun Alliance and London Insurance Group 1/214
Sunningdale Nurseries v-x; xvi; xv; xvi; xviii; 1/7; 1/9; 1/15; 1/16; 1/26; 1/32; 1/52; 1/64; 1/65; 1/71; 1/72; 1/77; 1/107; 1/117; 1/135; 1/138; 1/154; 1/161; 1/173; 1/184; 1/189; 1/191; 1/192; 1/195; 1/203; 1/207; 1/213; 1/222; 1/223; 1/228; 1/235; 1/249; 1/256; 1/257; 1/259; 1/278; 1/288; 1/293; 1/297; 1/306; 1/308; 1/313; 1/328; 1/329; 1/332; 1/339; 1/340;1/360; 1/372; 1/381; 1/415; 1/416;

1/417; 1/418; 1/429; 1/431; 1/443
Sutton Griffin and Partners 1/205
Sutton & Son Ltd 1/332; 1/415
Sutton Coalfield (Warks) 1/136
Sutton Hall (Yorks) 1/153
Sutton on the Forest (Yorks). 1/153
Suzuki, Hideo 1/224
— Takashi 1/224
Swedish Burial Ground 1/382
Swettenham (Ches) 1/234
Swinton Grange (Yorks) 1/33
Synge, Patrick M. 1/41
Syon House (Mddsx) 1/313; 1/328
Syon Lodge 1/385
Syon Park (Mddsx) 1/115

T. Hilling and Co Ltd 1/306; 1/339
Taaffe, G. 1/224
Tadcaster (Yorks) 1/346
Talbolt Manor (Norf) 1/457
Talbolt, Hon. Mrs T.G. 1/383
Tamlaght (Co Fermanagh, N Ireland) 1/111
Tamworth (Staffs) 1/116
Tarland (Aberdeen) 1/15
Tasmania 1/265
Taunton (Soms) 1/201
Taylor & Marr Ltd 1/289
Taylor, Jane 1/384
Taylour, Robert S. 1/385
Telston Nurseries 1/332
Temple, London, *see* London
Terrington (Yorks) 1/80
Terrington House (Yorks) 1/80
Terry, N.G. 1/386
Testbourne (Hants) 1/373
Tetbury (Glos) 1/465
Thelveton Hall (Norf) 1/268
Thenford House (Oxon) 1/210
Thirsk (Yorks) 1/206; 1/343
Thomas Rivers and Son Ltd 1/54
Thomas Rochford and Sons Ltd 1/35; 1/222; 1/347; 1/396
Thomas, Mr 1/222
— Graham S. vi; x; 1/9; 1/65; 1/126; 1/135; 1/138; 1/325; 1/329; 1/340; 1/359; 1/360; 1/365
—, Peter 1/387
Thompson, Sir Edward x; 1/342; 1/389
Thorp Perrow Arboretum (Yorks) 1/391
Three Gates House (Warks) 1/193
Tidcombe Manor (Wilts) 1/217
Tilehurst Potteries 1/336

INDEX OF PLACES AND PEOPLE

Tilhill Forestry (Crowborough) Ltd 1/191
Tilhill Forestry Ltd 1/332
Tillypronie (Aberdeen) 1/15
Timbers (Oxon) 1/192
Timsbury (Soms). 1/84
Tixall (Staffs) 1/48
Tixall Cottage (Staffs) 1/48
Tobermory (Argyll) 1/259
Tor, The (Berks) 1/78
Torksey (Lincs) 1/337
Toro Irrigation 1/171
Torosay Castle, Isle of Mull 1/215
Torrisdale (Argyll) 1/209
Towcester (Northants) 1/367
Tower Court (Berks) 1/372
Towneley, Simon 1/390
Trebor x; 1/24
Trefi Lodge (Mer) 1/17
Tregarne, Lady 1/110
Treharne, Prof J.K. 1/450
Trentagh (Co Donegal, Eire) 1/417
Trevor Smith, L.R. 1/222; 1/223
Trevor-Roper, Lady Alexandria 1/392
Tropic Flora Co. 1/315; 1/449
Truro (Cornw.) 1/236
Tsushi, Hiroshi 1/224
Tsuzuki, Fumiko 1/224
Tubesing, Charles E. 1/263
Tufnell, Maj. Timothy 1/394
Tunbridge Wells (Herts) 1/3
Turnford (Herts) 1/347
Turnford Hall Nurseries 1/35; 1/347
Tusting, John C. 1/395
Twyford (Berks) 1/163
Tyninghame (East Lothian) 1/173

U.S.A. xi; 1/151; 1/166; 1/290; 1/230; 1/290
Uckfield (Sussex) 1/200; 1/308
Uckfield House (Sussex) 1/308
Unique Dutch Light Co. Ltd 1/77; 1/165
Univerzitet Kirilli Metodii 1/446
Unusual Plants 1/90
Upcher, T. 1/397
Upton Grey (Hants) 1/304; 1/438
Upton Grey Place (Hants) 1/438
Upton Grove (Glos) 1/465
Urban Planters 1/171

Valley End (Surrey) 1/110
Van Oss, O. xv; 1/398
Van Tubergen Ltd 1/223; 1/228; 1/252; 1/400
Vandervell, Mrs 1/399
Vaughan, Viscountess 1/401
Venison, Tony 1/427
Verine Products and Co. 1/222
Vern, The (Heref) 1/117
Versepuy, see International Versepuy
Verulam, Earl of 1/402
Victoria (Australia) 1/414
Victoria Rd, London, see London

W.E. Chivers & Sons Ltd 1/20
Wagg, Jeremy 1/404
Walhurst Manor (Sussex) 1/83; 1/350
Walker, Maj. Patrick 1/405
— S.M. 1/405
Wall, B 1/448
Waller, Obby 1/348
Walmer, The Gothic House (Herts) 1/327
Walter Blom & Sons Ltd 1/222
Walton (Radn) 1/125
Walton Hall 1/368
Wantage (Berks) 1/256; 1/288
Wardhaugh, Mr 1/5
Wardley Hall (Lancs) 1/361
Warfield (Berks) 1/39
Wargrave (Berks) 1/54
Wargrave Manor (Berks) 1/54
Warminster (Wilts) 1/229
Warneford Place (Wilts) 1/142
Warren Cottage (Surrey) 1/387
Washington Palm Arboretum 1/446
Waterers Nurseries & Garden Centres xv; 1/381; 1/443
Waterers of Bagshot 1/328
Watford (Herts) 1/186
Watkins, Daphne 1/412
Watson, F. 1/213
— Katherine 1/413
— R.A. 1/391
Watson's Bookshop, Burford (Oxon) 1/413
Watt, Alistair 1/414
— Guy 1/442
Wealdon Woodlands Ltd 1/64
Webb, E.P. 1/202
Wedgewood, Hon. Josiah 1/415
  see also Josiah Wedgewood & Sons Ltd
Week-End Service 1/442
Weilin, Dr Chen 1/450
Weir, James 1/416

INDEX OF PLACES AND PEOPLE

— Mora 1/416
Weldon, Sir Anthony 1/417
Wellingham House (Sussex) 1/12
Wellshill Cemetery (Perth) 1/171
Wells-next-the-Sea (Norf) 1/99
Wemyss & March, Earl of 1/418
— Lady of 1/418
Wereham, Row Cottage (Norf) 1/273
Wernher, Lady Zia ix; 1/419
West, Lady 1/420
— Camilla 1/421
— David 1/442
— James 1/421
West Barsham Hall (Norf) 1/227
West Country Wildlife Park, The, Soms. 1/388
West Dean (Sussex) 1/41
West Midland Woodlands 1/197
Western Rosse, Scotland 1/72
West Woodhay House (Berks) 1/205
West Woodhay, The Old Rectory (Berks) 1/267
West Wratting Park (Cambs) 1/114
Westminster, Duchess of, Loelia xix; 1/253; 1/422; 1/424
— Duchess of, Sally 1/422
— Duchess of, Viola 1/423
Weston 1/398
Weston Hall (Northants) 1/367
Weston Marks (Hants) 1/304
Weston-under-Lizard (Staffs) 1/58
Wetherby (Yorks) 1/244
Weybridge (Surrey) 1/448
Whalton, The Manor House (N'land) 1/314
Whichford House (Warks) 1/340
Whichford, The Old Rectory (Warks) 1/340
Whitchurch (Hants) 1/430
Whitchurch (Berks) 1/38
Whithead, A. 1/222
Whitmee, Brian A.C. 1/425; 1/426
— Mrs B.A.C. 1/202; 1/425; 1/426
Whitsey, Fred 1/336; 1/427
Whittaker, Mrs 1/428
Whitwell Hall (Yorks) 1/152
Whitwell-on-the-Hill (Yorks) 1/152
Wicken House, The (Norf) 1/226
Wickenden Manor (Sussex) 1/15
Wickhambreaux (Kent) 1/297
Widcombe Manor, Soms. 1/472
Wiggins Teape Ltd x, xii; xviii; 1/18
Wilberfoss (Yorks) 1/440

William Duff and Son, (Forfar) Ltd 1/393
Willis, Mrs Victor (Peggy als Mrs Thomas Dunne) 1/202; 1/429
Wills, Hon. Patrick 1/430
Wilton, Earl of 1/431
Wilton Row, London, *see* London
Wimborne, Viscountess Venetia ix, xi; 1/442
Winch, Mrs 1/432
Windlesham (Surrey) v; 1/381
Windrush, The Old Vicarage 1/143
Windsor (Berks) 1/134; 1/328; 469
Windsor Great Park 1/365; 1/457
Wing (Beds) 1/25
Wingfield, Charles J. 1/434; 1/435
Winn, G. Mark D. 1/436
Wiseman, Mr 1/451
Wisley 1/328
   see also R.H.S. Wisley
Wivelsfield Green (Sussex) 1/187; 1/215
Woldringford (Sussex) 1/101
Wolfers, John 1/365
Wombwell, Beryl 1/437
— V. Malcolm 1/437
Wonersh (Surrey) 1/319
Wonersh House (Surrey) 1/319
Wonham Manor (Surrey) 1/196
Wood, Michael 1/438
— R.F. 1/377
Woodbridge (Suff) 1/326
Woodcock, A.F. 1/306
Woodhall Spa (Lincs) 1/195
Woods Landscapes 1/228
Woking (Surrey) 1/253
Worksop, Notts, 1/321
Wormald, Capt. R. 1/461
Wormersley House (Lincs) 1/195
Worsley (Lancs) 1/361
Worsley, Oliver 1/440
— Penelope 1/440
— Sir. Marcus 1/439
Worston (Lancs) 1/445
Worswick, Albert E. 1/458
Wright, Michael 1/396
Wrightson, Sir John 1/441
Wycliffe Hall, Durham 1/385
Wykeham, Angela 1/443
Wylye (Wilts) 1/44
Wynyate, F. 1/135
Wytherstone House (Yorks) 1/100

Yagi, M. 1/224

Index of Places and People

Yahiro, Kazuko 1/224
Yelverton (Devon) 1/144
Yenfeng, Dr Fu 1/450
York, Tadcaster Road 1/386
— University of xii; xv
— University of, Institute of Advanced
    Architectural Studies xv
Yorke, Susie 1/445
Young, A.J. 1/443
Younger, Mrs 1/444
Yovane, J. 1/323
Yugoslavia 1/446
Yvonne Arnaud Theatre xix; 1/253

Zetland, Machioness of 1/447
Zhenghou, Dr Jia 1/450
Zwanenburg Nurseries (The Netherlands)
    1/400
Zwijnenberg, P.G. 1/13